This book employs a simple rating system to help choose which places to visit:

✓	'top ten' sights

◆◆◆   do not miss
◆◆   see if you can
◆   worth seeing if you have time

INTRODUCTION

The Cypriot landscape is studded with hilltop monasteries and churches: this is Kykko Monastery, celebrated in the Greek Orthodox world

INTRODUCTION

The mere mention of Cyprus seems to stir the imagination. It is the third largest of the Mediterranean islands, stretching 149 miles (240km) from its west coast to its easternmost tip, and 60 miles (96km) from north to south; and the furthest east, lying close to the shores of Asia Minor. Perhaps it is this location at the crossroads of east and west, with its remarkable mixture of cultures and philosophies, that stimulates the imagination to create a make-believe picture of this distant land. Whatever it is, the reality is certain to be different from the imagined. One could not suspect that the lowly Kyrenia hills are much more spectacular than the high Troodos Mountains; or that the central plain is a barren dust-bowl in summer and an incredible blaze of wildflowers in springtime. People are surprised that the winter nights are cold and that vast amounts of snow fall on Mount Olympus and nowhere else. Any ideas that the villages are the well-kept counterparts of tidy western habitations will be quickly dispelled at first sight of the ramshackle collections of houses, picturesque as they might be.
The visitor might well be amazed that a jeweller

Essential Cyprus

by
ROBERT BULMER

Robert Bulmer was resident in Cyprus many
years, then returned to England to live. For him,
writing this book has re-established some
broken links with his favourite island.

Produced by AA Publishing

Written by Robert Bulmer
Peace and Quiet section
by Paul Sterry

Edited, designed and produced
by AA Publishing. Maps ©
The Automobile Association 1994

Distributed in the United Kingdom by
AA Publishing, Norfolk House,
Priestley Road, Basingstoke,
Hampshire, RG24 9NY.

Reprinted November 1995
Revised Third edition © The
Automobile Association 1994
Revised Second edition 1992
First published 1991

MAPS: The names printed on the
maps generally reflect those on
signposts and street signs. However,
alternative spellings, transliterated
from Greek script, are being
introduced in the south locally, eg
Ayios will become Agios, Paphos will
be Pafos, Yeoryios will be Georgios,
Larnaca will be Larnaka, Khirokitia
will be Choirokoitia, Ayia Napa will
be Aghia Napa and Palea Paphos will
be Palaia Perhaps.

A CIP catalogue record for this book is
available from the British Library.

ISBN 0 7495 0836 1

Published by AA Publishing, a
trading name of Automobile
Association Developments Limited,
whose registered office is Norfolk
House, Priestley Road, Basingstoke,
Hampshire, RG24 9NY.
Registered number 1878835.

Colour separation: L.C. Repro,
Aldermaston

Printed by: Printers Trento, S.R.L., Italy

Cover picture: Paphos (Pafos) harbour

This guide deals with all of Cyprus, a
divided land. Visitors should
appreciate that they must commit
themselves to either the Greek
(south) or Turkish (north) part for
their stay, as movement between the
two sectors is strictly limited to one
crossing-point from south to north
with return on the same day. Readers
interested in Greek Cyprus should
concentrate on the chapters
covering the Larnaca, Limassol and
Paphos areas; those wishing to visit
Turkish Cyprus should read the
Kyrenia and Famagusta sections.
Nicosia is partly in the Turkish sector
and partly in the Greek sector.

will repair his watch-strap for nothing and that the village garage man will stop everything to fix his tyre, at the same time sitting him down with a coffee or Coca Cola. This tradition of hospitality goes back hundreds and possibly thousands of years. In the villages food will be readily given, sometimes too much, and refusal cannot be contemplated. The visitor may also be surprised that in a Greek marriage the dowry system is operated, a house normally being provided (often at great sacrifice) by the bride's parents. This follows a chaperoned courtship, although western ideas are eroding this situation.

Even today, when the character of southern Cyprus's coastal strip has changed dramatically owing to tourist development, few people visit the island without falling under its spell. So what is it that visitors find so specially favourable? Is the country that much at variance with other Mediterranean lands? Well, there are differences in the landscape, though not dramatically so, and other islands do have fascinating antiquities, if not perhaps so many as Cyprus. It cannot be the beaches, Cyprus is not an island of endless sands along the shore. The weather is of course splendid, if a little hot in summer, and the sun shines for much of the year.

Even these considerable assets do not completely explain Cyprus's popularity. There is another factor – namely the people. The Cypriots have an advantage in that many of them speak excellent English, a throwback to colonial days. This gives them the opportunity to demonstrate to English-speaking visitors their friendliness and politeness, qualities they have in good measure. They are naturally gregarious and their knowledge of English adds to their confidence. If the visitor accepts Cypriot friendliness in a reciprocal spirit, then he can expect a welcome that seems almost too good to be true.

It should be noted that this description fits the Greek rather than the Turkish Cypriot. There are of course some great differences in language and religion. Nevertheless, the Turkish Cypriot has the same recent colonial history, so many speak good English. They are relatively shy and retiring compared with the Greeks, but

INTRODUCTION

even so are friendly, courteous and helpful. An enduring memory of north Cyprus is of the children, who rush to say 'hello' and 'goodbye' to any visitors in their village.

Unfortunately, the two communities no longer live side by side; they are separated by a military line that stretches from Pyrgos in the west to Famagusta in the east, and there is no escaping the presence of the military, especially in the north. For how this came about see **Background**, pages 9–12.

It has been said that holidays and politics should not bo mixed and it has to be conceded that most visitors to Cyprus are oblivious to the troubles. Nevertheless, the situation does impinge on them in one important respect. Visitors to the south can only enter the north at one point (see page 114) along the whole of the 85-mile (137km) demarcation line, and then they have to be back by 18.00 hours. Visitors to the north fare even worse. They are confined to this area and may not pass to the south. In fact although they may not know it, as far as the Republic (Greek-controlled Cyprus) is concerned (and only Turkey recognises the northern state), they are illegal immigrants, barred in theory for ever from the south. This book endeavours to cope with this unique complication as best it can.

The Greeks hold 62 per cent of the island and the Turks 37 per cent (1 per cent forms the buffer zone). There is plenty to see in either section. It may be that the very best of the scenery is in the north but in the south the sandy coasts of Ayia Napa and out west at Lara and Khrysokhou Bay are as good as any. The Turkish section does not have the equivalent of the cool Troodos Mountains, where numerous Byzantine churches are hidden among the pine trees of the valleys. In the south, Larnaca and Paphos are bustling holiday towns and Limassol a huge megapolis.

Because of the frenetic activity of the Greeks in recent years, many places have gone from small coastal villages to struggling towns, and the cities of Nicosia, Limassol and Larnaca are joined by fast modern highways. However, there are still some wild places out west by Lara and Cape Arnaouti and valiant attempts have been made by the action group 'Friends of Akamas' to restrict development in western Cyprus. The commercial forces ranged against them may be irresistible and only future years will show if they succeed or not. In any case, the difficulties are mainly on the coasts.

The pace of life in the north is noticeably slower. Muslim traditions and uncertainty about the future have dictated a gentle rate of progress. Little has changed since the aftermath of the Turkish invasion, in fact Kyrenia is now quieter than it ever was. Varosha, out in the east, is quietest of all, for nobody is allowed into this suburb of Famagusta.

On the hills the three great medieval castles of Buffavento, St Hilarion and Kantara still overlook the northern shores as they have done for centuries. In the west, the ruins of Soli and the Palace of Vouni receive a fraction of the visitors to Kourion in the Greek sector, as does splendid Salamis on the eastern seaboard. Nevertheless, there are signs that this accidental act of conservation, dictated by the magnitude of tragic events, may have run its course.

BACKGROUND

Any visitor who does not spend every minute on the beach must inevitably, sooner or later, encounter one of Cyprus's celebrated ancient ruins. Even in Ayia Napa, where most things are new, the Monastery is there to take one back 400 years. And in Paphos the journey back in time is much longer.

Should the traveller remain unmoved by all this ancient history, then the startling sight of United Nations soldiers holding the ground between the Greek Cypriot and Turkish military must raise a few questions of recent history. However, any explanation leads inexorably into the past and it soon becomes evident that the present trouble is one more chapter in the thousands of years of strife that Cyprus has endured.

Ancient and Medieval Cyprus

In fact we have to go back to Neolithic times to find a lengthy tranquil period. Cyprus existed in isolation at this time and the people lived quiet lives along

The ruins at Kourion bear witness to Cyprus's early importance

the north and south coasts in round domed houses. Khirokitia is the best known of their settlements. By the end of the Late Bronze Age (1600–1050BC) the island had emerged from its solitary existence and for the first time there was trade with Egypt, the Levant and Syria. Waves of immigrants arrived from Mycenae on the Greek mainland and established themselves along the coast. It was at this time that Cyprus's problems began, first with piracy and then domination by Phoenicians. Assyrians, Egyptians and eventually Persians.

The Romans annexed the island in 58BC and this marked the start of prosperous times. Many public buildings were built, including a gymnasium and theatre at Salamis and other theatres at Soli and Kourion. Several temples were also completed, including the Sanctuary of Apollo near Kourion. The splendid House of Dionysos and House of Theseus were built at Nea Paphos. Ruins of all the above buildings are clearly visible today.

Eventually the split in the Roman Empire resulted in Cyprus being ruled from Constantinople. The next centuries saw frequent attacks on coastal towns by Arab pirates and also invasions by more powerful Islamic fighting forces until Byzantium put the Arabs into retreat. In the 12th century the power of the Byzantines began to wane and Cyprus managed to become independent, albeit under the rule of the tyrant Isaac Comnenus. When Richard the Lionheart of England came to Cyprus in 1191 on his way to the Third Crusade, the course of history was dramatically changed. He defeated Comnenus in battle, but not requiring Cyprus as a possession he sold it on to the Knights Templar to raise money for the Crusade. The Templars found the island troublesome and asked Richard to take it back, which he did, although keeping the down payment. The benefactor was a knight called Guy de Lusignan, for Richard gave him the island. Though not a young man, Guy was a gallant soldier, and he established a lasting dynasty.

This kingdom of the Lusignans reached the height of its power under King Peter I, 1359–67. Fine examples of ecclesiastical architecture were built in Nicosia, Famagusta and the Karpas (Kirpasa), many of which remain today. With the passing of Peter I a rapid decline in Lusignan fortunes took place and the Genoese attacked the island and gained Famagusta. They were dislodged, but by now Lusignan authority had been irreversibly weakened and the way was open for a Venetian takeover in 1489.

Centuries of Conflict

Under the Venetians, Cyprus became an advance base against the expanding Ottoman Empire. With the threat of Ottoman invasion uppermost in their minds the Venetians constructed massive defences. Famagusta and Nicosia were encircled by the walls and

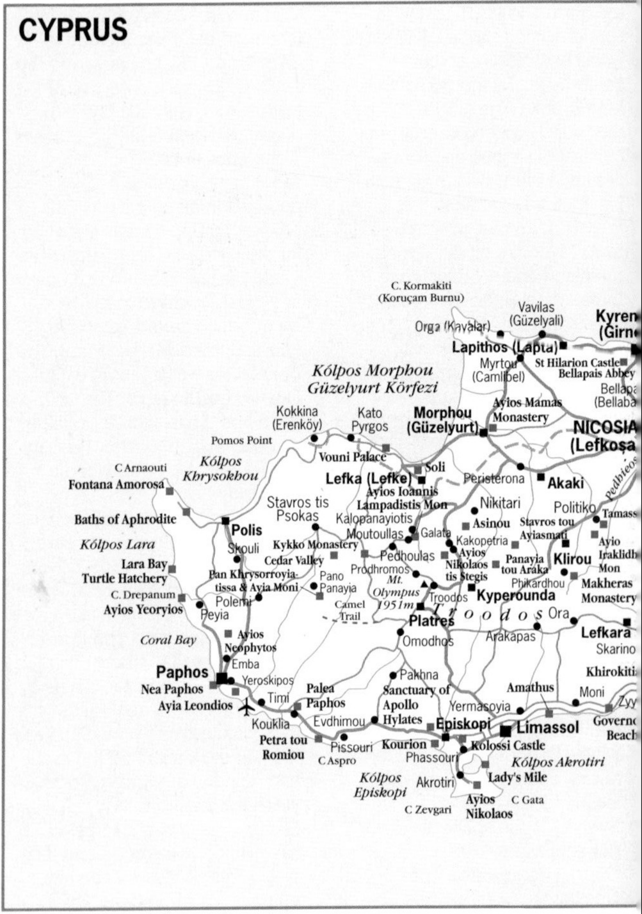

CYPRUS

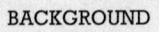

C. Kormakiti
(Koruçam Burnu)

Vavilas
(Güzelyali)

Orga (Kayalar)

**Kyren
(Girn**

Lapithos (Lapta)

Myrtou
(Camlibel)

St Hilarion Castle
Bellapais Abbey

Bellapa
(Bellaba

*Kólpos Morphou
Güzelyurt Körfezi*

Kokkina
(Erenköy)

Kato
Pyrgos

**Morphou
(Güzelyurt)**

Ayios Mamas
Monastery

**NICOSIA
(Lefkoşa**

Pomos Point

*Kólpos
Khrysokhou*

Vouni Palace

Lefka (Lefke)

Soli

Peristerona

Akaki

C Arnaouti

Fontana Amorosa

Ayios Ioannis
Lampadistis Mon

Nikitari

Politiko

Tamass

Stavros tis
Psokas

Kalopanayiotis

Asinou

Stavros tou
Ayiasmati

Ayio

Baths of Aphrodite

Moutoullas

Galata

Kakopetria

Iraklidh
Mon

Kólpos Lara

Polis

Skouli

Kykko Monastery

Pedhoulas

**Ayios
Nikolaos
tis Stegis**

Panayia
tou Araka

Klirou

Lara Bay
Turtle Hatchery

Cedar Valley

Prodhromos

Phikardhou

Makheras
Monastery

C. Drepanum

Pan Khrysorroyia-
tissa & Ayia Moni

Pano
Panayia

*Mt.
Olympus
1951m*

Troodos

Kyperounda

Ayios Yeoryios

Polemi

Peyia

Camel
Trail

T r o o d o s

Ora

Platres

Coral Bay

**Ayios
Neophytos**

Omodhos

Arakapas

Lefkara

Emba

Skarino

Yeroskipos

Palea
Paphos

Pakhna

Amathus

Khirokiti

Paphos

Timi

Sanctuary of
Apollo
Hylates

Yermasoyia

Moni

Zyy

Nea Paphos

Ayia Leondios

Evdhimou

Episkopi

Limassol

Governo
Beach

Kouklia

Petra tou
Romiou

Pissouri

Kourion

Phassouri

Kolossi Castle

C Aspro

*Kólpos
Episkopi*

Akrotiri

Kólpos Akrotiri

Lady's Mile

C Zevgari

**Ayios
Nikolaos**

C Gata

bastions that still surround the old sections of these towns. It was all to no effect, for a vast army of Turks stormed into Nicosia in 1570. Famagusta held out 10 months before surrendering in 1571.

Russia gradually became a threat to the Ottomans and in the event of an attack on Cyprus it was doubtful that they would be able to resist it. The Sultan of Turkey therefore in 1878 placed the administration of Cyprus in British hands. In World War I Turkey fought on the German side and as a consequence Britain annexed the island. In 1923 Turkey decided to renounce any claim to Cyprus

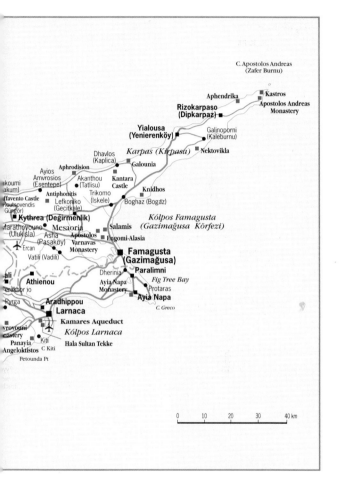

under the Treaty of Lausanne; Cyprus was then declared a British Crown Colony.

The local population had high hopes of an improvement in their situation under the British, but there was one smouldering problem – Hellenism. A dream of many Greek Cypriots was unification with Greece. Known as ENOSIS, it was a dream that made the Turkish Cypriot community fearful and was to lead directly to the division of Cyprus in 1974.

Remorselessly the idea gained momentum, and in April 1955 EOKA, a group of terrorists under the leadership of Colonel George Grivas, set off bombs throughout Cyprus. The real struggle for ENOSIS had begun, and the next years saw a bloody campaign against the British forces. There was a cessation of hostilities in 1959 leading to independence rather than ENOSIS. The Treaty of Zurich was signed in which Britain, Greece and Turkey guaranteed this independence of the new Republic from 16 August 1960. Under the terms of the treaty, Britain retains two Sovereign Bases at Dhekelia and Akrotiri-Episkopi. The constitution provided for dual Greek-Turkish government. The Greek Cypriot spokesman Archbishop Makarios became president with a Turkish deputy. Hostilities between the communities flared up in December 1963, however, resulting in the Turkish Cypriots eventually retreating into enclaves. United Nations

The castle and harbour at Paphos

soldiers were sent to Cyprus in the following year to keep the peace and they have been there ever since.

Resentments simmered and in 1967 hostilities between the communities were renewed. President Makarios was now seen as an obstacle to ENOSIS and there were attempts on his life by a revived EOKA (now EOKA B) under the control of Grivas. This culminated in the coup, supported by the military junta then in power in Greece, against Makarios in July 1974 and the election of a fanatical EOKA man, Nicos Sampson, as president. The triumph of EOKA was short lived, for five days later Turkish forces invaded to protect the safety of the Turkish Cypriot community.

A ceasefire and talks foundered and, on 14 August, Turkish forces took over northern Cyprus, about 37 per cent of the whole island. The division is known as the 'Green Line', a name which goes back to British attempts in the 1960s to separate Greek and Turkish communities, the boundary being delineated on the map of Nicosia in green ink. Talks between the two communities originally offered hope but ended in stalemate. The south prospered with tourism, and the north, hamstrung by embargoes and restrictions, stagnated. In 1983 the Turkish Cypriots unilaterally declared the independence of northern Cyprus, reinforcing the de facto partition. Further talks took place in 1985 and there were big expectations for the UN sponsored talks of 1992, but the stalemate persists.

LARNACA AND SOUTHEAST CYPRUS

The harbour at Ayia Napa

From the green foothills of the Troodos Mountains the land becomes white and arid around Larnaca, gradually giving way to the terrain known as the *Kokkinochoira*, a direct reference to the distinctive red soil of the agricultural east. Here windvanes pump water from below ground to produce early crops of Cyprus potatoes. The eastern shores are ideal for those wanting beaches close to hotels. However, apart from Larnaca (and Ayia Napa Monastery) nothing is old in the resort areas and Nicosia and Limassol are a full day out for people wanting a change of scene.

The beaches of Ayia Napa and the adjacent Nissi Beach are splendid and have attracted most of the holiday development. Now it has spread to the west for miles along the shore. It is the same story with Fig Tree Bay (Protaras) to the east; the beach is good for swimming and the calm waters attract water skiers (there is also plenty of accommodation and places to eat). Consequently, all beaches are now busy in the summer. Nearer to Larnaca, the beaches around the sweep of the bay are not as fine, although fringed by some good hotels. All of the area is quite accessible from Larnaca and its airport. Ayia Napa is 25 miles (40km), Fig Tree Bay is a little further. To reach either, one has to pass through the British Sovereign Base of Dhekelia. Any thought of a quick visit to seemingly nearby Famagusta should be quickly dismissed as the town is held by the Turks and access to the Turkish area is at one point only, in Nicosia.

LARNACA (LARNAKA)

Before the Turkish invasion of 1974 Larnaca was hardly known outside the island. However, with Kyrenia and Famagusta held by the Turks and Nicosia Airport controlled by the soldiers of the United Nations, the Greek Cypriots were suddenly without an airport and tourist industry. Within no time they had constructed an airport to take Jumbo jets, and hotels and apartment blocks sprang up on the shores to the east. So today, more than half of all visitors to Cyprus touch down at Larnaca and the world's sunshine charts list the town in preference to Nicosia. All this adds up to a town that is no longer as sleepy as it was; nevertheless it retains something of its old world air, a legacy from the days when all the foreign consuls resided there. It is not a place of beaches, the one small stretch of sand being man-made and turning a peculiar green at times. The seafront is a better place, its promenade lined with palm trees sporting distinctive beards. Places to eat abound and there are enough shops, plus a market.

Even in the hot sun of summer it does not take long to walk the short distance along the seafront from the **Marina** to the **Fort** at the southern end of the promenade. From here one can meander through old back streets and perhaps return along Zinonos Kitieos Street,

but first calling in at the church of **Ayios Lazaros**. There is a municipal zoo and gardens of no great merit and two museums. To the west is the **Salt Lake** and **Hala Sultan Tekke**. The latter is not within easy walking distance and is therefore covered in **What to See in Southeast Cyprus** (page 20).

Once a year, 50 days after Easter (Greek Orthodox Whitsun), the town becomes a fun-fair for the Feast of Kataklysmos (Festival of the Flood). The promenade disappears under lines of stalls and for two days throughout the afternoon and into the evening people crowd into the seas and sprinkle each other with water. This enjoyment of the sea with its ritual of sprinkling survives from ancient times and the festival is unique to Cyprus. The church has consecrated it in memory of Noah's salvation from the Flood, but underneath the blessing it is a pagan festival of lost origins. Many believe that it is a celebration of Aphrodite's birth, others her purification after union with Adonis. Nobody knows for sure and few care; they are simply happy to take part, sucking *soujoukko* or ice cream, and the bigger the crowd the more they enjoy it. Lutes and violins are played under the stars and even the ancient *aulos* (pipe) of Arcadia. Young men dance on timber platforms, re-creating the movements of their trade using sickles and milk churns.

There are music and poetry competitions, in fact the climax of the festival is the *Chattismata* or poetry battle. Competitors challenge each other in a game of instant repartee that can go on so long that it is impossible (or imprudent) to declare a winner.

One should not forget that Larnaca had a most distinguished citizen in Zeno, the founder of Stoic philosophy. This celebrity among all Cypriots was not a Greek but a Phoenician, born at Kition in 333BC. His portrait bust is displayed in something of a backwater at the junction of Nikodhimou Mylona Street and Leophóros Grigori Afxendiou. Away from the old town there is, with one notable exception, little of interest. Much of the area is residential with flat-topped buildings bristling with solar panels and water tanks and rusty steel reinforcing rods.

These last indicate that planning permission for expansion has been obtained, and, should such expansion ever take place, make further vertical construction a little easier. The one important exception is the ruins of ancient **Kition**, which, according to legend, was founded by Noah's grandson Khittim. There is not a lot surviving, but surely sufficient to make the short detour worth while, for it is here that one realises that Larnaca is a place with a history. It is built on the remains of this important city of antiquity dating from the 13th century BC.

As a resort, Larnaca can be considered as three separate areas. The town centre has a well established tourist district along the busy seafront road.

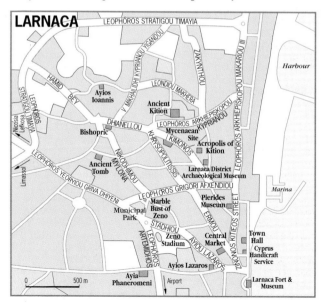

LARNACA

Cannon preserve the military aspect of the Turkish fort on the Larnaca seafront. Now a museum, the fort was erected in 1625

South of the town centre, another area, basically a wide promenade with shops and bars, lies fairly close to the airport. The third area, where most tourists stay, is well out of Larnaca on the Dhekelia road going north. This is a self-contained district of shops, cafés, restaurants and discos and many of the larger hotels with private beaches.

WHAT TO SEE

◆◆
ANCIENT KITION

starting at Kimonos Street
Ancient Kition is found northwest of the seafront. Once Kimonos Street is located progress becomes relatively straightforward. Most of the ancient city is buried under the modern town. Various artefacts from the site are kept in the Larnaca District Archaeological Museum (see page 17). At the north end of Kimonos Street is the **Mycenaean site**. There is not a great deal to be seen

today, but in 1962–3 a wealth of pottery, jewellery and alabaster vessels was discovered in tombs by a courtyard.
The **main site** of Kition is reached from Makhera Street. It is the most extensive of the discoveries made. A raised wooden gantry allows visitors a good view of the excavations. Early remains are of the 13th century BC and superimposed on them are the massive structures of a 12th-century BC Mycenaean settlement. The remains of the later city wall, built out of Cyclopean (very massive) blocks, are quite impressive, as are the remains of a large temple converted by the Phoenicians in the 9th century BC to a temple to Astarte. On the outer face of the south wall crude images of ships can be detected.
Open: (main site) 07.30–13.30

hrs Monday to Saturday, June to September; 07.30–14.00 hrs October to May (on Saturday closes an hour earlier). The other sites generally have unrestricted access although new excavations are often closed to visitors.

◆◆◆
AYIOS LAZAROS

Ayios Lazaros Square
Built by Emperor Leo VI in the 9th century, this is an unusual and interesting church, all the more so because the white-painted belfry somehow survived a Turkish ban on campaniles. The Turks were ever fearful of rebellion and considered it possible that the Christians would use the high towers to signal the start of an uprising.

According to legend Lazaros was resurrected by Jesus, but promptly expelled by the Jews of Bethany to arrive in Cyprus where he definitively died and was buried. In 890 his tomb was discovered and his remains sent to Constantinople only to be later removed by the French and sent to Marseilles.

The original church dates from this time and was used by the Turks for a short period in the 16th century. Some time in the 17th century the church was rebuilt and the large campanile was added.

Four domes cover the central nave, although they are not visible from below, and the roof is supported on four double piers. In one of them a rococo pulpit is ingeniously built, on another a silver filigree icon of 1659 depicts the passing of

Lazaros. The saint's empty sarcophagus is found under the sanctuary, near the south apse. At the south entrance the royal doors carry Byzantine and Lusignan coats of arms. Outside the northwest corner is an English cemetery.

◆◆
LARNACA DISTRICT ARCHAEOLOGICAL MUSEUM

Kimonos Street/Kilkis Street on Kalogreon Square
The museum is northwest of the seafront. Inside the garden are a circular mosaic pavement and some column capitals. On entering the building one sees immediately a collection of sundry limestone torsos and terracotta figurines. There are many ceramic finds from Kition. Among other interesting artefacts are bronze tools, weapons, vases and mirrors. *Open*: 07.30–13.30 hrs June to September; 07.30–14.00 hrs October to May (on Saturday closes at 13.00 hrs). Closed on Sundays. Tel: (04) 630169.

◆◆◆
PIERIDES MUSEUM

4 Zinonos Kitieos Street
This museum occupies a mid-18th-century house that until the fighting of 1974 was shared with the Swedish Consulate. The collection was gathered together in 1839 by Demetrios Pierides, a man of Venetian ancestry. Members of his family shared his enthusiasm for the collection and later added to it. Inside, there are four rooms exhibiting such items as terracotta statues from the ancient city of Marion and

medieval glazed pottery. Some of the early maps of Cyprus displayed are of interest.
Open: 09.00–13.00 hrs Monday to Saturday. Tel: (04) 622345.

◆◆◆
LARNACA FORT AND MUSEUM
Ankara Street (on the seafront)
This building dates from 1625. In the early days of British rule it was used as a prison and barracks. Now it houses objects from Kition and the Hala Sultan Tekke excavations (see page 20) and ancient cannons lie in the corner of the garden. In summer the open courtyard is fitted with seats for folk dancing performances.
Open: 07.30–19.30 hrs Monday to Saturday, June to September, closes at sunset October to May.

Accommodation
Larnaca is something of a problem for the independent traveller. There are good new hotels galore around the bay, but these are all package deal places, though some have rooms vacant out of season. In Larnaca itself it is tough going and the unwary or desperate could end up in a mosquito-ridden bordello. In the hope that this is avoided a few hotels are listed below.
La Maison Belge, 103 Stadio Street (tel: (04) 654655). There are 16 nicely carpeted rooms and breakfast is included in the moderate price. 1-star.
Pavion, 11 St Lazarus Square (tel: (04) 656688). The 10 rooms have private showers and optional air-conditioning. 1-star.
Anesis, 150 yds from beach near the town centre (tel: (03) 721104) 2-star; 62 rooms.
Karpasiana Beach Sunotel, Larnaca-Dhekelia road, Orkolini (tel: (04) 655001). Large and modern with 111 rooms, out of town around the bay. 3-star.
Beau Rivage, Larnaca-Dhekelia road (tel: (04) 623600). A typical modern design of 188 rooms overlooking Larnaca Bay. 3-star.

Nightlife
For those who like *bouzouki* music there is the **Golden Night** club at 25 Galileos Street, and the **Nostalgia** on Leophóros Stratigou Timayia. Visitors may also wish to try the **Fantasia Cabaret or** the new **Chitquito**, both on Leophóros Stratigou Timayia. There is also the **Atalanti** night-club. The **Prince of Wales** bar and the **Meeting Pub** are two drinking spots. Around the bay the modern hotels generate their own entertainment with barbecue evenings and Greek dancing.

Restaurants
Larnaca's restaurants have little to offer those wanting a rewarding gastronomic experience. However, worth a try are:
Alakati, near the Larnaca Fort, south of seafront (tel: (04) 653042). A family-run restaurant serving good *meze*.
Militsis, also near the Larnaca Fort and serving good *meze*. Both are popular with locals.
Napa Castle, Ayia Napas Avenue (tel: (03) 721697). Cypriot fare and Steaks.
To Dichorio, near south end of Zinonos Kitieos Street. Charcoal grill and Cypriot specialities.

Shopping

Many of the shops are on Zinonos Kitieos Street just back from the seafront. Some of the brasswork is good: watch out for ashtrays, candlesticks and engraved boxes. Carpets and curtains are in oriental patterns, sheepskin and goatskin rugs are everywhere.

WHAT TO SEE IN SOUTHEAST CYPRUS

◆

AQUEDUCT

1¾ miles (3km) west of Larnaca
The aqueduct is on the Limassol road. Also known as Kamares, it was erected in 1745 by the Turks to bring water to Larnaca. Altogether there were three sections adding up to 75 arches; only 37 remain today. In 1939 it was abandoned.

◆◆

AYIA NAPA (AGHIA NAPA)

25 miles (40km) east of Larnaca
This is a modern town of hotels, apartments and discotheques. The heart of what was quite recently a sleepy old place barely survives, protected by a 16th-century Venetian monastery (see below), which lies on the south side of the village square surrounded by a high wall.

Accommodation

Some suggestions are:
Savvas Apartments on the road to Paralimni. Write to PO Box 240 (tel: (03) 721187). Studios and one- and two-bedroomed apartments – 10 in all.
Nick's Apartments in centre of new town. Write to PO Box 40

Savvas Apartments in Ayia Napa. Many visitors prefer the freedom of apartment accommodation

(tel: (03) 721621). 20 modern flats with a total of 40 beds.

Restaurants

There is a similarity in the fare offered in restaurants but there are also a number of quick takeaways selling kebab in pitta bread and of course hamburgers. Some hotel restaurants are open to non-residents and the barbecue evenings can be good.
Worth a try are:
Costaros, on the road west to Nissi beach. Good Greek food at a reasonable price. Popular with locals.
Fish Harbour, by the harbour. Serves excellent fish *meze*. Not too expensive.
Marcos, by the monastery. The Greek food is good.
Blue Lagoon, in the village centre. Offers an international menu at moderate prices.

SOUTHEAST CYPRUS

Stavrovouni Monastery, high on its peak, has dominated the country all around for over 1,650 years

◆◆◆
AYIA NAPA MONASTERY
Ayia Napa Village

The monastery turns an almost blank façade to the village centre. This is a design feature that the Venetian architects could never have imagined would be so useful 400 years later, for it enables the monastery to remain a place of peace and tranquillity amid the general hubbub. To the south it is a little more open but the once magnificent sea view is now cut out by new buildings.

The monastery was completed just before the Turkish occupation of 1570. Inside, it is very pleasant with a cloistered courtyard and some finely carved windows. In the centre of the courtyard is a beautiful octagonal fountain, complete on each side with a high relief of garlands, coats of arms and animals' heads. The feature is surmounted by a large dome carried on four pillars. There is another fountain with water gushing out of a carved boar's head, on the north side of the courtyard.

The complex is now used as a conference centre by the World Council of Churches and it is open to the public.

◆◆◆
HALA SULTAN TEKKE (also TEKKE OF UMM HARAM) ✓

3 miles (5km) west of Larnaca on the road to Kiti

The dome and minaret of the Tekke can be seen among palm trees on the west bank of Larnaca's Salt Lake. In summer it is a haven from the blistering reflected heat of the salt flats. It is here, so legend has it, that Umm Haram, the foster mother of the Prophet Muhammad, is buried. She broke her neck in a fall from her mule when travelling with her husband during an Arab raid on Cyprus in 647. This makes the Tekke an important place of Muslim pilgrimage, surpassed only by the shrines of Mecca, Medina and al Aksha (Jerusalem). Two great upright stones carrying a stone lintel were used to mark the burial place. The sanctuary is now enclosed by a dome constructed in 1760. The octagonal mosque with its restored minaret stands in cool shady gardens by a fountain. Shoes must be left outside. *Open*: daily 07.30–19.30 hrs June to September. The shrine is closed at sunset during the rest of the year.

◆◆◆
PANAYIA ANGELOKTISTOS
Kiti Village
The village is seven miles (11km) southwest of Larnaca on the road that passes the airport. The church is a few steps to the north of the village crossroads. The key is in a house near by. Angeloktistios means 'built by angels'; in fact most people refer to the building as Kiti Church. It is thought that the church was built at the beginning of the 11th century on the ruins of a 5th-century basilica. Although the architecture is impressive in its own right the church is more famous for the outstanding mosaic within.
It is found in the central apse

and will be lit up on request. The Virgin Mary stands on a jewelled footstool attended by angels. In her left arm she holds the Christ Child, and the archangels Gabriel and Michael stand to the side. The design is of extreme delicacy. Historians cannot agree on the date of the mosaic but it is certainly much older than the church and possibly belongs to the 6th century.

◆◆◆
STAVROVOUNI MONASTERY
about 25 miles (40km) west of Larnaca, off the Nicosia–Limassol road
The monastery, perched on an eyrie 2,257 feet (688m) above sea-level, is visible from far around. All the fun of getting up the mountain's hairpin bends has now been taken away by the new road. One can of course walk up the ridge to the summit. Once at the monastery the views of Larnaca in the east and the Troodos Mountains to the west are quite spectacular. The monastery was founded in 327 after St Helena, the mother of Constantine the Great, brought a relic of the true Cross from Jerusalem (Stavrovouni means 'Mountain of the Cross'). A supposed fragment of this is covered by a silver casing and set into a 500-year-old cross draped in damask and encased in beaten silver. Arabs destroyed much of the original building in 1426 and the remainder was burned by the Turks in 1570. In the 17th century the monastery was re-populated by Orthodox monks. Many of the present monks have

Café society on Nissi beach. The Ayia Napa area is well endowed with safe, sandy beaches

lived here for decades, and are extremely devout. Privileged visitors may be shown a collection of skulls, lit up suddenly and dramatically by the sun's rays. These skulls of dead monks are stacked on shelves with their names inscribed on their foreheads. Women, unfortunately, are not allowed inside the monastery. Men may visit daily from sunrise to sunset, except between 12.00 and 13.00 hrs (15.00 hrs in summer) and not at all on Green Monday (see page 104) and the day following.

Beaches

Some of the finest sandy beaches on the island lie at least 20 miles (32km) east of Larnaca, in and around Ayia Napa. In normal conditions there are no big waves and the beaches gently shelve. Waterskiers need to get up early before the daily breeze sets in although flat calm returns in late afternoon. For them the best runs and selection of boats and gear are at the modern resort of **Protaras** at the southern end of Famagusta Bay, 10 miles (16km) from Ayia Napa. The beach here, **Fig Tree Bay**, is excellent with soft golden sands around a fig tree. **Nissi** beach just to the west of Ayia Napa has a small rocky island and is excellent as is the beach of **Ayia Napa** itself. A little further west are smaller beaches just as good. Windsurfers will find a good breeze at times. Much closer to Larnaca, at the southern end of the bay, the developers have turned an ordinary strip of shore into a reasonable beach, although it does not compare with the sands of Ayia Napa and Fig Tree Bay.

The beaches have attracted an abundance of hotel and apartment development. **Kiti beach** seven miles (11km) south of Larnaca sees fewer visitors, although incredibly some tourist development is finding a foothold on this somewhat unexciting coast. The shingle beach is a favourite with the locals – a row of holiday homes has sprung up immediately to the west. There are some trees for shade and the shore shelves fairly steeply. From Larnaca the route is past the airport, turn left at Meneou and generally head towards the sea on newish roads.

LIMASSOL AND THE SOUTH COAST
Cape Kiti to Cape Aspro

This area takes in the foothills of the Troodos Mountains and nearly 100 miles (160km) of coastline, including the Akrotiri peninsula. Much of the shore is a strip of shingle, the only good beach east of Limassol being **Governor's Beach**. To the west things improve and the sands of Evdhimou and Pissouri by the

Fishing boats and yachts share the old harbour at Limassol

great white cape (Cape Aspro) are excellent. On Akrotiri Bay to the south of Limassol, a stretch of sand called **Lady's Mile** makes a four-mile (7km) sweep to Cape Gata.

There are scores of ramshackle villages in the valleys of the vine-covered foothills, most notably **Lefkara** in the east. As one would expect the coastal strip has not been overlooked by the tourist industry, although most of the development is concentrated on Limassol, spreading far along the city's east coast road.

Limassol is cut off from Nicosia and the central plain to the north by the high Troodos. These mountains are the reason why it is the centre of the wine industry, for the south-facing terraced slopes are ideal for growing vines.

LIMASSOL

On the Cypriot time-scale, Limassol is young. When Richard the Lionheart landed near by in 1191 it was not much more than a village. He was

Limassol's Wine Festival takes place every September

inhabitants and has been its main industrial town since long before tourism. Wines, spirits, beer and soft drinks are produced, vegetables and fruits are canned, cement, bricks and tiles are made. The ships in the huge port west of the town deliver these goods world wide. In testimony to the importance of its wine industry Limassol's September Wine festival is a merry affair. Nevertheless, the carnival in spring is more spectacular (see page 105).

WHAT TO SEE

◆
FOLK ART MUSEUM
253 Ayiou Andreou Street
Cypriot folk art of the 19th and 20th centuries are displayed. Exhibits include national costumes, embroidery and tapestry.
Open: 08.30–13.00 Monday to Saturday, also 16.00–18.00 Monday, Wednesday and Friday (15.00–17.00 October to May).

◆◆
LIMASSOL CASTLE – CYPRUS MEDIEVAL MUSEUM
Eirinis Street, near Old Harbour
For all its size and importance Limassol has few sites of antiquity. The castle is the only one of any note and even this is merely 600 years old, although the remains of earlier Byzantine fortification can be seen in some of the walls. The chapel in which Richard the Lionheart and Berengaria may have been married in 1191, is no more, and the central pillar supporting the vaulting of the Great Hall of the

seasick and in a bad humour; however, he cheered up to marry Berengaria of Navarre, in **Limassol Castle**, and crowned her Queen of England. Limassol is now a town of painted hotels and apartment blocks that reach along the coast to Amathus and beyond. However, the success of Limassol as a tourist centre owes less to its mediocre beaches than to its concentration of swimming pools, shops and nightlife. Amazingly, relics of the old town of poets and artists are still there, and the old harbour still shelters small fishing boats. Limassol is the island's second largest town with 115,000 castle collapsed in 1525. Later, when the Turks took over, they made it into a redoubt. Very much later it became a gaol, and some time after 1940 it was the British Forces headquarters. The castle stands in a pleasant garden north of the old port and customs house. Steps climb up to the north entrance and to the right is the Great Hall. A spiral stair continues on the roof with views over the town. Artisans' shops line the surrounding streets, in the grounds is the Cyprus Medieval Museum. *Open*: 07.30–18.00 hrs Monday to Saturday, June to September (until 17.00 hrs the rest of the year). Tel: (05) 330419.

◆

LIMASSOL DISTRICT ARCHAEOLOGICAL MUSEUM
Kaningos-Lordos Vyronos corner, near the Municipal Gardens
It contains displays of axeheads and tools of the Neolithic period, Bronze and Iron Age ceramics and Mycenaean pottery; also amphorae and statuettes . The jewellery is impressive and

so is a bronze bull. Make certain of seeing the statue of the Egyptian god Bes from Amathus (325BC) and the headless Zeus holding an eagle (4th century). *Open*: 07.30–18.00 hrs Monday to Saturday (17.00 hrs October to May), 10.00–13.00 hrs Sunday.

Accommodation
Curium Palace, 2 Byron Street, near Gardens and Zoo (tel: (05) 363121 or write to PO Box 48). A pleasant hotel, older than the new crop of establishments, with pool and friendly staff. 4-star.
Chez Nous Sunotel, Potamos Yermasoyias area on a side street. Comfortable reasonably priced 2-star, with pool.
Limassol Palace, 97–9 Spyros Araouzos Avenue (tel: (05) 352131 or write to PO Box 3186). A small hotel on the seafront. 1-star.
Miramare, Potamos Yermasoyias (tel: (05) 321662 or write to PO Box 521). A large hotel of 190 rooms right by the shore. Located between the old town and the development of recent years. 4-star.

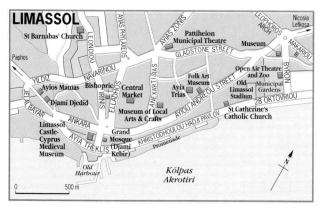

Apartments

Olympia Management & Services Bureau are able to offer a variety of self-contained accommodation from studios to three-bedroomed apartments in the town's main tourist areas.

Their central office is at Limassol Centre Building (1st floor), 2 Rigas Fereos Street, PO Box 4017 (tel: (05) 365774/364665).

Nightlife

There is plenty of nightlife in Limassol – the massive influx of visitors sees to that. It seems that the centre of this activity is now in the area known as Potamos Yermasoyias, a little to the east of the old town. Many hotels and most tavernas have their own live band and visitors are encouraged to join in the fun and try a few steps of Greek dancing. The larger hotels have their own discothèques but there are some independent ones too. Naturally there are several night-clubs; the **Archontissa** is found on Makariou III Avenue and the **Alexandra** on the Nicosia road. Maxim cabaret is located on Stassinou Street.

Restaurants

Neo Phaliro, Gladstone Street, Old Town (tel: (05) 365768). Greek food popular with locals.
Assos, Old Limassol road (tel: (05) 321945). Famous meze and local dishes.
Aphrodite's Garden at the Sir-Criso Hotel (tel: (05) 321411).

Street fish market in Limassol

Busy Bodies, east of Limassol near Amathus Beach Hotel. Good, varied food and not too expensive.

Camares Flambé Restaurant, Limassol–Nicosia road (tel: (05) 321573).

Ladas Fish Restaurant, 1 Sadi Street (tel: (05) 365760). The seafood here is as good as anywhere.

Shopping

The old town offers the best shopping near Ayiou Andreou Street. This quaint street, not far from the seafront promenade, is a cornucopia of small speciality shops. There is even a Marks & Spencer housed in a pleasant old building with balconies.

WHAT TO SEE FROM CAPE KITI TO CAPE ASPRO

◆◆

KHIROKITIA (CHOIROKOITIA)

near present-day Khirokitia (20 miles (32km) northeast of Limassol)

The Neolithic site is found between Larnaca and Limassol, a little west of the new dual-carriageway where it turns north for Nicosia. One should watch out for the signs to be able to leave the highway in good time. Visitors from Larnaca should stay on the old road.

Khirokitia was discovered in 1934 and the settlement is the earliest found so far in Cyprus, possibly extending as far back as 6800BC. A characteristic feature of the houses is that they are all beehive shaped. Foundations were smooth rounded river stones and the superstructure was of mud bricks. It is clear that the buildings were occupied over a considerable period for there are several superimposed floors carrying hearths, seats and round tables and platforms.

Graves were dug in the floors, and gifts of stone vessels and personal ornaments deposited in those of the women. A heavy boulder placed on the chest of some of the buried indicates a fear of the dead.

The excavated part of the settlement lies mainly on the south slopes of the hill and partly at the saddle connecting it with other hills to the west. A long wall structure, in reality a street, starts by the river, near the present bridge, and climbs the slope before changing direction to pass through the settlement to the northwest.

The buildings nearest to the entrance to the site belong to this middle period. Towards the centre of the site are buildings of the third period.

You have to ascend to the top of the hill to find dwellings of the first period of the settlement. There is a large house of alternate stone and mud bricks and also a smaller house where 26 burials were discovered. At the top of the slope are more round houses and a view over the upper reaches of the river and carob-dotted hills beyond.

Open: daily 07.30–19.30 hrs (closing at sunset from October to May).

◆◆◆

KOLOSSI CASTLE

Kolossi village 8 ½ miles (14km) west of Limassol

The castle is impressive and the cypress trees and gardens are

THE SOUTH COAST

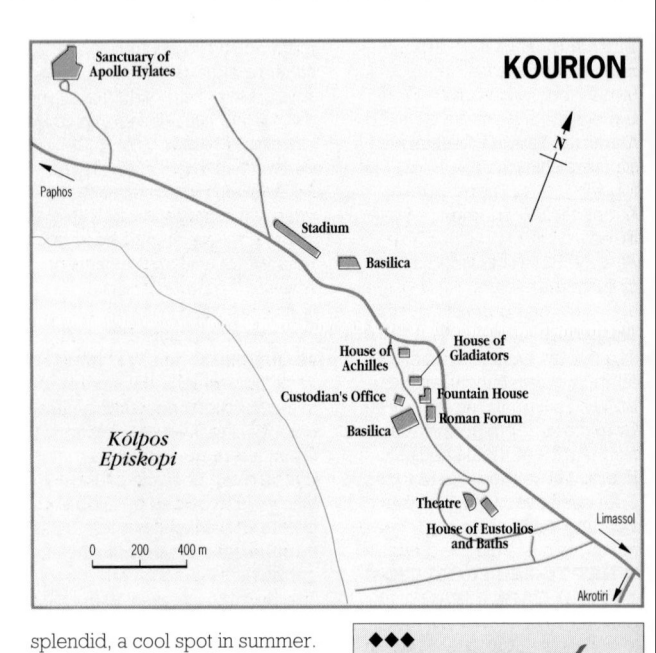

splendid, a cool spot in summer. The Knights Hospitaller were granted land at Kolossi by King Hugh I in 1210 and they built a castle, although not the one we see today. When Acre fell in 1291 the headquarters of the Order moved to Limassol then on to Kolossi, and the Grand Commandery of Kolossi became renowned as the richest possession of the Knights.

The original castle suffered much damage in the Genoese attacks and the lands were ravaged by the Mamelukes in 1425–6. All this led to the rebuilding of the castle in the mid-15th century, and the conspicuous square keep dates from this time.

Open: daily 07.30–19.30 hrs (closing at sunset from October to May).

◆◆◆
KOURION (CURIUM) ✓

12 miles (19km) west of Limassol
This impressive site is on high cliffs overlooking the waters of Episkopi Bay, on the road to Paphos. Kourion comes second only to Salamis as an archaeological site worth a visit. The time to go is early morning, before the heat of the day and when the sea below is a flat calm. The area has been inhabited since Neolithic times. There are indications that colonists settled here during the first wave of Mycenaean expansion in the 14th century BC, others following in the 12th century BC. The city played a vital role in the rebellion against the Persians in 498BC. To judge by the visible remains, Kourion remained a place of importance

until the later Ptolemaic and Roman administrations.

Like all the coastal cities of Cyprus, Kourion suffered at the hands of Arab raiders, so much so that in the 7th century the cliff-top site was abandoned and Kourion declined into insignificance.

The road from Episkopi passes close to the site and climbs the hill to the high part of the cliffs. This is the only convenient access and it is where the Custodian's office is located. It must have been here where the **Paphos Gate** stood although nothing remains. Near the office is the **House of Achilles**. This had an open courtyard with rooms either side and a colonnaded portico. A mosaic is set in the pavement of the portico and depicts Achilles disguised as a maiden, unwittingly revealing his identity to Odysseus. A smaller panel in an adjoining room represents Ganymede being carried off to Olympus by an eagle.

It is thought that the building was a reception area for important visitors and that it dates from the 4th century AD. A short way into the site is the **House of Gladiators**. Its name refers to the two gladiators locked in combat depicted in the colourful mosaic of the courtyard.

Close by are what is left of the **Aqueduct** dating from the Roman period, and one of two bringing water to the city in terracotta pipes from far-away springs. It was built in stone and was perhaps 18 feet (5.5m) high, sufficient to pass over the city walls. The water was directed to the **Fountain House** and stored in cisterns for the public to draw on.

A little further on to the right is the **Basilica**. Enough remains of the 5th-century building to indicate that it was of impressive size. The track ends on a northern slope which would have led to the **Amathus Gate**. Here on a fine site overlooking the coast, the sloping ground was used to good effect and the Graeco-Roman **Theatre** was built. It was excavated in 1949–50 and reconstructed in the 1960s. A vaulted corridor runs around the back from which five gangways enter the curved auditoria. There are seats for 3,500 people. Today there are public performances of ancient Greek dramas, Shakespeare plays and music concerts during the summer months, events generating a tremendous atmosphere. Details are available from the Tourist Offices.

The **House of Eustolios** is found higher up the slope than the theatre and a little to the east. It is a palatial building and was constructed after the abandonment of the theatre. There are some mosaic floors, completed in the early part of the 5th century. Entrance was to the west through a vestibule. An inscription in the mosaic floor welcomes the visitor: 'Enter and good luck to the house.' Inside, there is a rectangular garden court with porticoes on three sides. Other rooms extend to the south and east.

Initially the annexe was a private residence, becoming a place of public recreation when the mosaic floors were laid. Steps climb northwards to a higher level and the **Baths**. The central room has a mosaic floor with four

exceptional panels; one shows a partridge (much photographed) and one the female bust of Ktisis, a personification of the Creation. Off the central room is a *frigidarium* (cold bath) complete with foot baths and to the west a *tepidarium* and a *caldarium* (hot bath), the latter with built-in basins (some have survived).
Open: daily 07.30–19.30 hrs (closing sunset October to May).

The Stadium

This is not on the headland site but ½ mile (1km) along the road to Paphos, reached by a track on the inland side of the road.
The outline of the U-shaped plan is preserved, as are the outlines of the three entrance gates, one on either side and one in the middle of the rounded end. A section of seating has been reconstructed to show the original layout. There are seven tiers which accommodated about 6,000 spectators.
The stadium was built in the 2nd century AD during the time of the Antonine emperors and remained in use until about 400.
Open: daily 07.30–19.30 hrs (closing sunset October to May).

Sanctuary of Apollo Hylates

This is a little further on the road towards Paphos than the stadium, in all about two miles (3km) from the main site.
Here is one of the chief religious centres of ancient Cyprus. Apollo was worshipped as God of the Woodland (Apollo Hylates) and protector of the city of Kourion. The site excavations revealed that this worship began as early as the 8th century BC and continued to the 4th century AD. There were several rebuildings

and the existing remains are from about 100 AD, replacing earlier works destroyed by earthquake in 76–7. These later buildings were themselves destroyed by earthquakes in the 4th century. Several walls, found lying flat as they had fallen, have been re-erected.
Ancient worshippers entered the sanctuary through the Kourion Gate from the east, or the Paphos Gate from the west. However, the present-day visitor approaches from the south, skirts the main building and passes through the remains of the Paphos Gate.
Close to the Kourion Gate is the **Votive Pit** where the priests disposed of unwanted objects dedicated to the sanctuary. A narrow pavement now leads north to the ruined **Temple of Apollo** (1st century), partly restored. It was a small building, the rituals taking place usually in the open air.
A return to the pavement and the long portico of the South Building brings a flight of steps descending into the **Palaestra**, on the Kourion Gate site.
Athletes used the colonnaded central court of the Augustan period for exercise and games. No doubt the big stone water jar in the corner of the court was used for washing down and cooling off. However, if the athletes wished to bathe in style they would use the **Baths** on the other side of the approach to the Kourion Gate. Here cold tanks were available at the end of a long hall. A succession of warmer rooms led to the hottest of all, next to the furnace.
Both the Palaestra and Baths are outside the sanctuary proper, as

The mountain village of Lefkara, famous as a lace-making centre

can be seen by the remains of the enclosure wall.
Open: daily 07.30–19.30 hrs (closing sunset October to May).

◆
KOURION MUSEUM
Episkopi village, 8¼ miles (14km) west of Limassol
The collection, kept in a beautiful old house, was started by an American archaeologist in 1937. On display are terracotta chariots, lamps, figurines and limestone heads plus many other ancient artefacts.
Open: daily 07.30–13.30 hrs

Monday to Saturday, June to September; 07.30–14.00 hrs Monday to Friday, 07.30–13.00 hrs Saturday, October to May.

◆◆◆
LEFKARA
30 miles (48km) northeast of Limassol
The village is more or less equidistant from Limassol, Nicosia and Larnaca. From the Limassol–Nicosia highway, exit 13 (Skarinou), the route through the hills is five miles (8km) long. Visitors on the fast highway should keep a good lookout for the signpost, those on the winding road can be a little more relaxed. Lefkara stands high in the eastern

THE SOUTH COAST

Troodos at 2,400 feet (730m) above sea-level. Drivers should not be deterred by the climb for the road is not especially difficult. There are two Lefkaras, Pano and Kato, meaning high and low. Pretty as the villages are they have a greater claim to fame (especially the higher village). Lefkara is known world-wide for its hand-made lace (*lefkaritika*) and needle embroidery. It is made by the womenfolk and they can be seen working in the courtyards off the narrow alleyways, using a skill that is passed on from mother to daughter; a cottage industry that has existed for hundreds of years. None other than Leonardo da Vinci is reputed to have bought a quantity of lace for Milan Cathedral when he visited Cyprus in 1481.

In addition to lace Lefkara produces *loukoumia* or 'Turkish Delight', which is worth sampling, and with luck visitors may also see it being made.

The **Lace and Silverware Museum** in the House of Patsalos is open all year Monday to Saturday 10.00–16.00 hrs.

Beaches

Curium

The beach lies below the ancient cliff-top site of Kourion (Curium) 10 miles (16km) west of Limassol. It is a long expanse of sand not normally very busy. A serious drawback is that part of the beach, indicated by the red buoys, is dangerous to swimmers at all times.

Evdhimou

This is an excellent beach in lovely country 17 miles (27km) west of Limassol. It gets its name from Evdhimou village, three miles (5km) inland. The sand is excellent, as is the swimming. At the eastern end is a small jetty and the usual café.

Governor's

This fine beach 14 miles (22km) east of Limassol has sharply cut white cliffs of modest height. It would therefore be reasonable to expect the sand to be white, but astonishingly it is black or nearly so. Consequently it absorbs heat and becomes extremely hot.

The beach, although narrow, is very popular with the Cypriots who travel miles to get there at weekends. On the cliff-tops are collections of crudely built holiday chalets.

Lady's Mile

Visitors will find the beach immediately south of Limassol, beyond the large port area. Watch out for the blue sign. There is a lot of sand here, nevertheless it cannot be described as a good beach. The surroundings let it down. Pylons stand inland on the British Base of Akrotiri.

Some 2½ miles (4km) east of Limassol at Dhassoudi, the Cyprus Tourism Organisation has created a public beach with various facilities.

Accommodation

There are a few hotels in the Cape Kiti area including:

Faros village, Perivolia village, 8½ miles (14km) southwest of Larnaca (tel: (04) 422111). A modern development with 136 rooms. 3-star.

3 Seas, Perivolia village (tel: (04) 422901). A modern hotel with 52 rooms. 2-star.

PAPHOS AND WESTERN CYPRUS

This part of Cyprus is perhaps a little greener than elsewhere and generally a little cooler than the eastern parts.

The foothills of the Troodos Mountains run down to the western shore and there are some spectacular views over the sea, especially in the late afternoon when the burning sun is reflected in the hazy blue distance. In the summer evenings the sunsets themselves are memorable, with the sun daily sinking in a cloudless sky, with absolute predictability.

The town of **Paphos**, famous for its ancient ruins, is the only centre of any consequence on

The goddess Aphrodite is said to have been born from the sea-foam here at Petra tou Romiou

the western seaboard. To the north, a little inland from the shore of Khrysokhou Bay is the large and sleepy village of **Polis**. Paphos is an ideal starting place for exploring this part of Cyprus. However, the unspoilt coast of the Akamas peninsula requires a jeep, as beyond Cape Drepanum there is only a rough track. **Lara** beach is excellent and it is here that the loggerhead and greenback turtles crawl up the sands to lay their eggs. These ancient creatures are under threat despite the valiant efforts being made to safeguard them.

Out east the terrain is unspectacular until **Petra tou Romiou** (the Rock of Aphrodite) comes into sight (15½ miles (25km) east of Paphos). Here the land turns white, and the coast road inland and all the valleys lead into the high

Troodos. The monastery of **Panayia Khrysorroyiatissa** sits 2,000 feet (610m) up in the wooded hills while much lower down near Paphos is the impressive monastery of **Ayios Neophytos**.

To the north Khrysokhou Bay sweeps majestically eastwards from Cape Arnaouti to Pomos Point. It is ringed by hills and retains some greenery even in high summer. Polis stands a little inland and does its best to ignore the increasing number of tourists driving up from Paphos.

PAPHOS (PAFOS)

Although at times in antiquity the island's capital, Paphos has, until recent times, been something of a western outpost – certainly in terms of tourism. All this changed when the floodgates were opened with the building of Paphos airport. The town is now quite large after considerable building and still growing along the coast.

It has to be said that the beach of Paphos itself is a miserable affair, but the harbour with its Turkish fort is splendid. Here there are restaurants and snack bars, a resident pelican, plus a turtle farm near the sea wall. In the latter turtles are nurtured to self-dependence and then released on the western shores in a last-ditch attempt to prevent their extinction. At the back of the harbour, by the lighthouse, is a Roman theatre and many of the archaeological sites for which Paphos is justly renowned (see **What to See**).

In ancient times the town around the harbour was called Nea

(new) Paphos (and more recently Kato, or lower Paphos). This was to distinguish the town from the older city of Paphos twelve miles (19km) east. To complicate matters further the part of Paphos which sits on the rocky plateau overlooking the lower town is called Ktima. This need not be the headache it sounds and visitors may simply refer to Paphos in all cases. Once there was a clear separation between the two parts but today this has been swallowed up by the new shops, hotels and apartment blocks. Modern buildings and important archaeological discoveries now sit side by side.

In the evening Paphos throws off its slumber and comes alive, with visitors thronging the streets to find their favourite restaurant or bar, or merely promenading down to the harbour.

The upper town (Ktima) should not be ignored. It has some substance to it and is charming enough with shops, churches, some interesting government buildings and a somewhat bustling air these days. Despite temptations it tends to leave tourism to its coastal sister and generally concerns itself with agriculture and the marketing affairs of this prosperous region.

WHAT TO SEE

◆
BYZANTINE MUSEUM
Elysee Street, in the old town
This is a small collection of exhibits from Byzantium. They are mainly of religious works and include icons and wood carvings.

The Paphos pelican is a popular resident of the harbourfront, where eating places abound

Open: 09.00-13.00 and 16.00-19.00 hrs Monday to Friday (afternoon times 14.00-17.00 hrs from October to May), 09.00-13.00 hrs Saturday.
Tel: (06) 232092.

◆◆
ETHNOGRAPHICAL MUSEUM
1 Exo Vrisy Street, near the Bishop's Palace
This private collection is the result of the enthusiastic work of Georges Eliades over the years. At his own expense, and in his own house, he has gathered together axeheads, coins, amphorae, farm implements and kitchen utensils. There is a reconstructed bridal chamber with interesting costumes and

furniture. In the garden are two tombs of the 3rd century BC.
Open: 09.00-13.00 and 16.00-19.00 hrs Monday to Saturday (except afternoons, 15.00-17.00 hrs in October to April); 10.00-13.00 hrs Sunday.
Tel: (06) 232010.

◆◆◆
NEA PAPHOS
The ruins are extensive but mainly contained within Kato (lower) Paphos and the scrub land to the north of the harbour. The route followed here starts in the area of Leophóros Apostolou Pavlou, and moves south to eventually reach the harbour. From here the ruins to the west and north are systematically covered. Admission times where applicable are given at the end of this section.

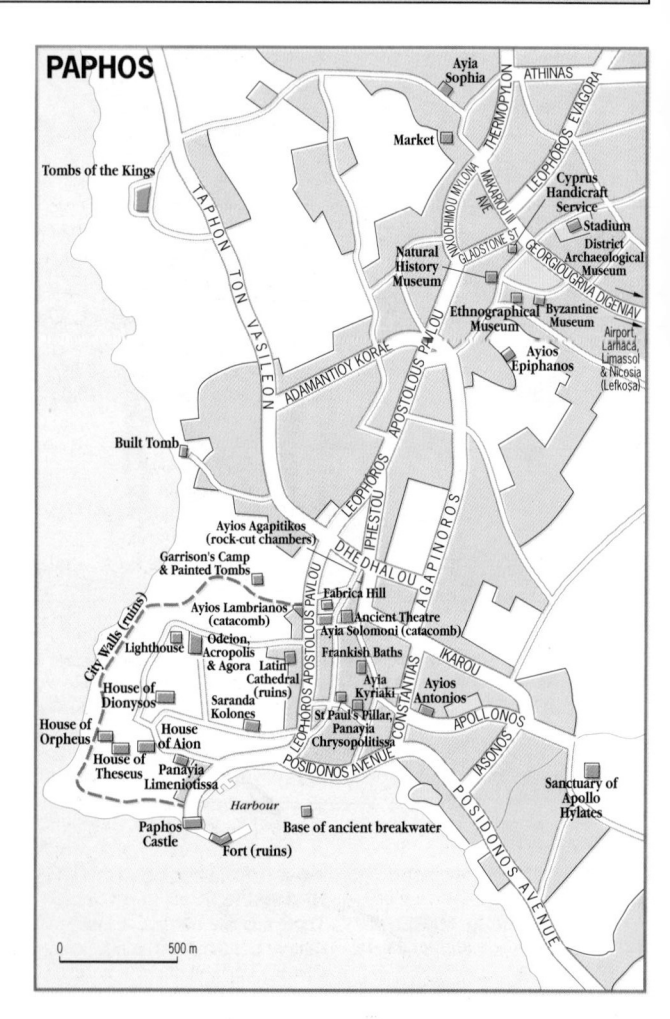

PAPHOS

Underground Churches (Catacombs)

These had pagan beginnings before being dedicated to Christian Saints. They straddle Leophóros Apostolou Pavlou. **Ayia Solomoni** on the east has underground chambers off an open court with a chapel of the 12th century. The apse has a (damaged) fresco, Crusaders being the first to deface it with their names. A flight of steps leads to a holy well. To the west of the road is **Ayios Lambrianos**, similar but not fully excavated.

St Paul's Pillar and Panayia Chrysopolitissa

A shattered column stands by the Church of Chrysopolitissa (Ayia Kyriaki) east of Leophóros Apostolou Pavlou. Legend has it that St Paul was bound to the pillar in the year 46 and given 39 lashes for preaching Christianity. Later, undeterred, he did better and converted the Roman governor, Sergius Paulus.
The church dates from the 13th century. A belfry was added to the Byzantine design.

Early Christian Basilica

Extending over much of the site that accommodates the later church of Chrysopolitissa (see above), east of Lephóros Apostolou Pavlou, are the ruins of this 4th-century basilica, one of the largest early Byzantine basilicas on the island. Some of the mosaic floors have survived.

Byzantine Castle (Saranda Kolones)

Across Leophóros Apostolou Pavlou and 220 yards (200m) to the west is the castle. Built in the first years of Lusignan rule, it sits on a mound overlooking the harbour. Before excavations began in earnest in 1957 there was only a pile of broken columns; the site is known as the 'forty columns'.

Fort

Right by the harbour is one of two *Kastillia* built by the Lusignans as a defence against seaborne attack. The central Frankish tower was dismantled by the Venetians at the time of the Turkish invasion of 1570, for they were unable to defend it

and did not want to leave it to the enemy. In 1580 the Turks restored and strengthened the fort, the work being described in the inscription over the main entrance. Steps down lead to dungeons, steps up to the roof with views over the harbour.

Mosaics ✓

The mosaic floors of the Houses of **Theseus**, **Dionysos** and **Aion** (3rd-century noblemen's villas) are among the finest in the Eastern Mediterranean and are magnificently preserved.

House of Theseus

A little inland in the direction of the lighthouse and 500 yards (457m) from the harbour, are the ruins of this Roman residence. It takes its name from the circular mosaic floor representing Theseus slaying the Minotaur. This is found at the east end of the atrium. Another mosaic shows the Birth of Achilles.

House of Dionysos

The Roman villa dates from the 3rd century and is close to the House of Theseus. Superb well-preserved mosaic floors are the attraction. Ganymede and the Eagle is depicted along with Dionysos, the God of Wine, being carried in a chariot. Mosaics of Apollo, Daphne, and Pyramos and Thisbe are equally impressive.

House of Aion

This is the smallest house, discovered in 1983. There is one large mosaic with five scenes one of them Leda and the Swan.

City Wall

Much of the wall can be traced but the better part lies to the northwest in the region of the lighthouse. Here it was cut from the rock. Access to Nea Paphos used to be from the sea, through the northwest gate, the position of which is identified today by a stone ramp. Towers stood at each side of the gate.

Roman Theatre (Odeion)
The theatre stands close to the lighthouse, an impressive semicircle 156 feet (47.5m) in diameter. It was built in the 2nd century but what we see today is a reconstruction, for the earthquakes of the 4th century did terrible damage. Yet it continued to be used for another 300 years until Arab raids forced its abandonment.

Tombs of the Kings
The tombs are out on their own 1¼ miles (2km) north of the harbour. They form the northern extremity of the necropolis of Nea Paphos. There is nothing royal about them and their popular name may relate to their grand appearance.
The tombs, which are of the 3rd century BC, are entirely cut into the rock, as are the steps down. There are steep drops at the edges of the tombs and extreme care should be taken when walking around them.

Many of the sites are not fenced or controlled. However, the Houses of Theseus, Dionysos and Aion and Tombs of the Kings are, and the admission times are as follows: daily 07.30-19.30 hrs (07.30 hrs-sunset, October to May).
The Paphos Fort times are: 07.30-13.30 hrs Monday to Saturday in June to September; 07.30-14.00 hrs Monday to Friday, 07.30-13.00 hrs Saturday in October to May.

◆◆◆
PAPHOS DISTRICT ARCHAEOLOGICAL MUSEUM
Dighenis Street
The museum's collection continues to grow as further excavations at Nea Paphos are carried out. Note the Hellenistic sarcophagus, unearthed a few years ago at nearby Peyia. There are the usual terracotta figures and statuettes and some coinage of the city kingdom. The worn marble torso is a Graeco-Roman sculpture of Aphrodite found in the sea off Paphos. A collection of marble eyeballs is intriguing as are the clay hot-water bottles fashioned to the shapes of feet and hands. Other artefacts come from the House of Dionysos and House of Theseus at Nea Paphos. (see page 37).
Open: June to September 07.30-13.30 and 16.00-18.00 hrs Monday to Saturday, 10.00-13.00 hrs Sunday; October to May 07.30-14.00 and 15.00-17.00 hrs Monday to Friday, 07.30-13.00 and 15.00-17.00 hrs Saturday, 10.00-13.00 hrs Sunday. Tel: (06) 240215.

Accommodation
Most tourists stay in the modern resort area to the east, about 1½ miles (2.5km) from the town centre. Most of the hotels are new and geared up for holiday packages. Certainly, out of the high season, independent travellers will usually be able to find accommodation in many of these hotels. They are generally

of a high standard.

Cheap hotels are not plentiful but unlike some of the other towns most are acceptable, if a little basic. Below are a few examples.

Aloe, Poseidon Street (tel: (06) 234000 or write to PO Box 190). A large modern hotel with 112 rooms, 3-star.

Axiothea, 2 Hebes Malioti Street (tel: (06) 232866 or write to PO Box 70). A family-run hotel with 37 rooms, many with a balcony and sea view. 2-star.

Dionysos, 1 Dionysos Street (tel: (06) 233414 or write to PO Box 141). A modern hotel with 94 rooms. 3-star.

Pyramos, 4 Ayios Anastasia Street (tel: (06) 235161 or write to PO Box 444). 20-room hotel with some good singles. 1-star.

Fine floor mosaics are the glory of the Roman villa at Nea Paphos known as the House of Dionysos. This one depicts the god with Ariadne

Apartments
Land of the Kings. Offers studios, and one- or two-bedroom apartments in the historic Tombs of the Kings Road (tel: (06) 241770 or write to PO Box 368).

Nightlife
In Paphos eating out takes up most of the evening and then there is the regular stroll down to the harbour. Most of the hotels put on entertainment for their guests and a few have discothèques that run into the early hours.

Restaurants
Some of the *kentrons* under the vines by the roadside provide marvellous local food at a medium price. Do not, however, always expect modern comforts such as lavatories.

Some restaurants worth a visit are as follows:

In Paphos, restaurants provide a relaxed atmosphere

Edelweiss, Limaniotissa Court, Ayiou Antoniou Street (tel: (06) 235885). An excellent restaurant with an adjoining bar.
Esperides Garden, 28 Posidonos Avenue, Kato Paphos (tel: (06) 238932). Excellent Cypriot and international cuisine.
Raffles, Tomb of the Kings Road (tel: (06) 2488519). International cuisine with tasteful surroundings.
Savvas Café Restaurant, Marina Court, Poseidon Street (tel: (06) 236225). A varied menu at reasonable prices.
Alex Fish Tavern, Kato Paphos. Excellent fish *meze* at reasonable prices.

Shopping
Kato Paphos has numerous souvenir shops, all selling the same goods. Much on sale is of poor quality, but some of the local handicrafts in basketware and leather merit consideration. Various well-stocked supermarkets provide for those staying in apartments.
The traditional Cypriot shop- and stall-holders are found up on the hill in the old town. If peckish, try the locally produced *loukoumi* (Turkish or Aphrodite's Delight), a sweet almond confection that is usually sampled with Turkish coffee. The public market on Agora Street, with its fresh fruit and vegetables, is an attraction. Go on Saturday morning.

WHAT TO SEE IN WESTERN CYPRUS

♦♦♦
AKAMAS ✓

Until recently few people visited this peninsula or even knew it existed. This is not quite the case today and the debate is how to preserve it untouched. It is an area of outstanding beauty, 60sq miles (155 sq km), with hills, some quite spectacular, running down to a rocky shore with delightful sandy coves. Turtles still come ashore here to lay their eggs. The flora includes some unique Mediterranean species. Cape Arnaouti lies at its northern extremity but is too far to walk to in the heat of summer. Take a boat from Lachi and ask to be dropped off along the shore and return on foot. Leave your car at the Baths of Aphrodite and a boatman will make a pick up from the beach below. Failing this, it means a taxi from the Baths back to Lachi.

♦♦♦
AYIA PARASKEVI

Yeroskipou Village, 2 miles (3km) east of Paphos
The church, in the centre of the village, is not only picturesque, but is as interesting as any of the Byzantine churches of Cyprus. A feature of the vaulted basilica is the way three domes over the nave intersect with two over the aisles, thereby forming a unique Byzantine cross. Inside the southeast corner is a square chapel, possibly a mausoleum in earlier days. The church was enlarged in the 19th century and again in more recent times,

mercifully withstanding these assaults on its integrity. Decorations over the altar date from the 10th century. Some paintings date from the 10th century and there is a 12th-century Dormition of the Virgin. However, most of the paintings in the nave are 15th century including the double-face icon of the Virgin Mary.

The village itself is probably of Byzantine origin. Signposts in the centre direct one to a **Folk Art Museum** a short distance away. Despite its attractions some visitors to Yeroskipou claim that its most important offering is the *loukoumi* (Turkish Delight) that is readily available.

Admission to Folk Art Museum: 07.30-13.30 hrs Monday to Saturday, June to September; 07.30-14.00 hrs Monday to Friday, 07.30-13.00 hrs Saturday rest of year. Tel: (06) 240216.

♦♦♦
AYIOS NEOPHYTOS

5½ miles (9km) north of Paphos
The monastery, set at the very end of the road that goes through Emba and Tala, is an interesting complex that comes dramatically into view as the road turns into the upper section of a wooded valley.

Most of the older buildings round the courtyard are of the 15th century. A flight of steps leads up to the church, a building of three aisles with a barrel-vaulted roof carried on columns. In the apse are sections of a 16th-century mural and there are older ones in the aisle vaulting. Some icons of the same period have survived. In a wooden sarcophagus are the saint's bones, and his skull is in a silver receptacle.

The monastery was founded in the year 1200 by Saint Neophytos from Lefkara, who lived for 40 years in a cave he cut in the rock, calling it his *Encleistra* (enclosure). Visitors will see it opposite the church, together with the cave-chapel of the Holy Cross and another cave. The walls and ceilings are decorated with paintings, many of them carried out under the supervision of Neophytos .

◆◆◆
KHRYSORROYIATISSA MONASTERY (PANAYIA KHRYSORROYIATISSA)

1 mile (1.7km) south of Pano Panayia

Paphos is the nearest town to the monastery. About 10 miles (16km) along the road to Polis is a turn off right to Polemi leading in nine miles (14km) to **Pano Panayia**, (the birthplace of Archbishop Makarios), now a museum. The monastery was founded by Ignatius the Hermit in 1152 and is set in an exceptional landscape of wooded hillsides and splendid views. The present church is from 1770 (restored in 1955) and has a unique triangular cloister. Within is an icon depicting the Virgin Mary; covered in silver leaving only the face visible. There is a collection of Holy Books and manuscripts.

◆◆◆
PALEA PAPHOS (PALAIA PERHAPS)

12 miles (19km) east of Paphos

Palea (old) Paphos is the original Paphos, founded 1,200 years before the Paphos we know today on the western seaboard. The ruins are found on a flat-topped limestone hill rising from the coastal plain in the village of Kouklia. It is an extensive area and it can be seen that the passing centuries have not been kind to the once great city. A solid well-built Turkish manor house marks the main entrance to the site and is the museum building.

With Salamis in the east of the island Paphos always held a place of special importance among the ancient kingdoms of Cyprus. Its claim to fame sprang from its sanctuary. According to legend Aphrodite had risen from the sea at Petra tou Romiou near by, and the temple subsequently constructed became the most famous of Aphrodite's shrines in antiquity.

Paphos reached the high point of its development in the 7th-4th centuries BC, but with the founding of Nea Paphos, possibly in 321BC, there grew up a serious rival to the old city. Kouklia village stands on part of the site of Palea Paphos. By all accounts the inhabitants were slow to lose the age-old pagan cults and until recently young women practised fertility rites by the church of Khrysopolitissa (Katholiki) near the sanctuary. From the top of the flattened hill there is a fine view of the coast to the south. To the west exist extensive ruins of Roman origin. Over in the east the city wall runs along the ridge. In the shallow valley below is a necropolis. Outside the city wall to east and west are extensive cemeteries from the 11th century BC to late

Roman times, most of them now covered up.

Manor House (Museum)

The main entry to the site is at the Manor House. Of the original Château de Covocle only the east and south wing survive; the north wing and gate tower, the west wing and half the east wing are Turkish. The building has been partially restored and serves as a museum and storerooms for artefacts from the site. Steps lead from the existing courtyard to the level of the medieval one. Here is a cross-vaulted hall, lit by small pointed windows. It is one of the finest surviving monuments of Frankish profane architecture on the island. There is a fine view from the room above.

Originally the manor was a fortification and was damaged by the Mamelukes in 1426. In the hands of the Turks it was extended and became the *chiftlik,* or manor house of a farm. *Open*: daily 07.30–19.30 hrs (07.30 hrs to sunset from October to May).

Sanctuary (or Temple) of Aphrodite

This is found a little way east of the museum. Surprisingly the goddess was not, as elsewhere,

Inside Khrysorroyiatissa Monastery: the silver-coloured icon of the Holy Virgin is its chief treasure

represented as a human figure, but as a conical stone, which was anointed with oil at the festivals.

Roman Remains

Some 440 yards (400m) west of the sanctuary is the **Roman Peristyle House**. It was built in the 1st century and later reconstructed. Various rooms are grouped round the colonnaded atrium. Mosaics of geometric pattern are preserved in the peristyle. Further to the northwest is the **House of Leda**. Here the mosaic pavement of the *triclinium* (summer dining room), dating from the late 2nd century, was found almost completely preserved. Leda and the Swan are depicted in it.

Christian Remains

The **Katholiki church** (formerly Panayia Khrysopolitissa) is found within a small ruined cloister close to the temple ruins. In Byzantine days the church served the village which stood around the ruins of the ancient kingdom. There is a dome over the intersection of the simple cruciform plan. Most of the building is of the 12th century but the west arm is a later edition. The ruins of the small 16th-century Byzantine church of **Ayios Nikolaos**, lie northwest of the sanctuary.

Defences

To the northeast of Kouklia village (on the way to Arkimandrita), is **Marcello Hill** and the site of the **Northeast Gate** and the **siege works**. The gate occupied a commanding position above the city. Excavations have revealed elaborate siege and counter-siege works.

◆◆
PANAYIA CHRYSELEOUSA
2 miles (3km) north of Paphos
Panayia Chryseleousa sits in the middle of the village of Emba. It is a simple 12th-century structure, originally of the cruciform type and complete with dome. There are many paintings in various states of preservation.

◆◆
POLIS
overlooking Khrysokhou Bay, 23 miles (31km) north of Paphos
There are signs that one day Polis, with its fishing refuge of Lachi, will become a tourist centre. At present it is a quiet old place, a good example of a Cypriot village. In 1875 it had a population of about 100, now it is nearer 2,000. By the shore is an official campsite under the trees (see page 110).

Close to the village is the location of ancient Marion. It was founded in the 7th century BC by the Athenians and did well out of copper until destroyed by Ptolemy in 312BC. A new town was built adjacent and called Arsinoe after the sister of one of the Ptolemies, Polis being a name that was first used in Lusignan times. Surrounding the area is a necropolis and hundreds of tombs. Over the years these have yielded numerous ancient relics.

Beaches

Coral Bay
Two bays cut into white cliffs in

A quiet cove west of Polis. This part of the coast is as yet largely untouched by mass tourism

fine country, eight miles (13km) north of Paphos. The sand is excellent and the sea beautiful. Despite the distance from Paphos it is rapidly becoming a place for those wanting a busy beach and plenty happening. There are sunbeds, motor boats and soaring paragliders, and hotels now over-look the white sands.

Kissonerga
This is a good stretch of sand among the banana plantations, about four miles (6.5km) north of Paphos on the way to Coral Bay. It looks a developer's paradise.

Khrysokhou Bay
The bay sweeps eastwards from the western snout of Cyprus with vast stretches of sand. West of Polis the beach by the **Baths of Aphrodite** (complete with tourist pavilion) is a good spot. The baths themselves are a spring in the woods near the pavilion, a cool place in summer. High ground all round contributes to the fine scenery. Further west is **Fontana Amorosa**. It is not a beach but nevertheless is a place on which the official tourists literature waxes eloquent. In fact few people seem to get there. The fountain itself is a muddy well, although Cape Arnaouti where it is situated is a splendid place. Visitors from the Paphos area should go towards Polis and turn west near Prodhromi. Access is by jeep or boat, for the road is too rough for cars. To the east the beach is not as good, has

quite a bit of shingle and seems somewhat straight and boring. Things improve at Pomos Point and beyond. It is really a question of taking your pick of the three or four beaches in this area.

Lara

This is a wonderful area on the west coast with excellent beaches either side of the headland. The approach road, once the best dirt track on the island, has been ruined by the British Army and is now terrible. However, the good news for the visitor is that they can take a boat from Paphos; these run most days in summer. Unfortunately this is bad news for the turtles, Lara beach being one of the last refuges in the Mediterranean for the loggerheads and greenbacks to lay their eggs. It is also the island's only home for the Mediterranean monk seal. In recent years the authorities have tried to protect the animals. A hatchery was established by the headland although there is no certainty that visitors will see turtles there.

Petra tou Romiou (Aphrodite's Rock)

The rocks are 15½ miles (25km) east of Paphos on the way to Limassol. Undoubtedly they are an impressive sight and whether you believe that Aphrodite really did emerge from the foam here hardly matters. It is generally a question of a quick dip in the blue sea from the shingly beach, for there are strong and strange currents around the rocks, also the main road is close by and brings too many sightseers for

real comfort.

Up on the cliffs is a tourist pavilion for refreshments and a good view of the rocks. These are worth a visit at any time but in the late afternoon the light can be memorable.

Timi

Timi beach is directly south of Timi village to the east of Paphos. No one would claim that it is the best of watering places, but it is not bad, and free as yet of hotels. The sand is good and a collection of little bays is very much to the liking of local people at weekends.

At Yeroskipou (between Timi and Paphos) there is a Tourism Organisation beach complete with changing rooms, bars and restaurants.

Accommodation

Bunch of Grapes Inn (tel: (05) 221275). In Pissouri village, 20 miles (32km) east of Paphos. A completely restored 100-year-old inn maintaining all the traditional features and with 9 guest rooms each with private bathroom. It is situated in the middle of the village at a height of 1,000 feet (300m) above sea-level and three miles (5km) from the beach. Also has an interesting courtyard restaurant. **Elia Latchi Holiday Village** at Lachi near Polis (tel: (06) 321011). 98 flats.

Restaurants

In Coral Bay resort, about eight miles (13km) north of Paphos is the **Corallo** restaurant (tel: (06) 221052) serving excellent food at sensible prices. There are other good places adjacent.

FROM NICOSIA TO THE HIGH TROODOS

The suburbs of Nicosia lie amid olive groves between the rugged Kyrenia Hills to the north and the Troodos Mountains to the south. In summer the spectacular Kyrenia range is a hazy backdrop of blue and grey monotones, but on a clear winter's day the peaks stand out in sharp relief. This part of the central plain is a splendid siting for a capital city. In this section our southern boundary is the natural barrier of the high ground of Troodos, the northern one the 'Green Line', that bisects Nicosia on its way from Famagusta to Güzelyurt Körfezi (Morphou Bay) and beyond. Nicosia marks the eastern end of the section, Kykko Monastery the west. Despite its distance from the main holiday centres Nicosia receives many visitors, one reason being the old walled city, which makes a visit especially worthwhile.

Some miles to the west, the village of **Peristerona** merits a call because of its domed church of Ayii Varnava (Barnabas) and Hilarion. Further into the Troodos foothills **Asinou Church** (Panayia Phorviotissa) is more than worth a detour, especially for its interior. Nearer to Nicosia is the ancient site of **Tamassus**, a good place for a picnic. In contrast to the sharp ridges and rocky cliffs of the Kyrenia mountains, the Troodos massif presents a friendlier face. The hills are rounded and the more uncultivated areas are covered in pine forest. Innumerable valleys cut deep into the mountain flanks but a sharp escarpment is not to be found and ramshackle villages perch

Artistic riches glow inside the 10th-century church of Ayii Varnava and Hilarion at Peristerona

on all but the highest ground. Unlike the lowlands there are few flat roofs because of the heavy winter rains. Snow falls on the highest ground and Mount Olympus sees skiing from January to the end of March. Around Platres on the southern slope of Olympus a few nature trails have been created. Pleasant as they are they will hardly satisfy walkers looking for wild open space. However, farm tracks and forestry roads abound, and walkers should try the hills south and west of Palekhori in the eastern hills. It is useful to know that the temperature in the mountains is still likely to be in excess of 26°C (80°F) in summer, and the sun is even more ferocious. In winter the hills see a lot of cloud and rain.

Many Cypriots spend their summer holidays in the mountain villages to escape the enervating heat of the lower ground. These are officially listed as 'Hill Resorts', a description that seems to suggest that they are more sophisticated than the reality, for the facilities are somewhat limited.

Even so, for the passing visitor, **Kakopetria**, off the main Nicosia-Troodos road is a good stopping-off place, as is **Platres** over the mountain-top on the descent to Limassol.

From Nicosia the scenic route up to Olympus is via Kalopanayiotis, Moutoullas and Pedhoulas and on to Prodhromos (see page 63).

If the coastal regions of Cyprus are richer in ancient sites and antiquities, the mountains come out best in ecclesiastical matters with their monasteries and painted Byzantine churches. From **Makheras Monastery** in the east, a sprinkling of interesting churches is dotted through the high valleys all the way to **Kykko Monastery** in the west. These monasteries are refreshingly cool in summer. A distinguishing feature of the Byzantine churches is the double pitched roof of clay tiles supported on timber rafters. This is merely a weather protection for the dome within.

Makheras Monastery is magnificently situated in the high Troodos

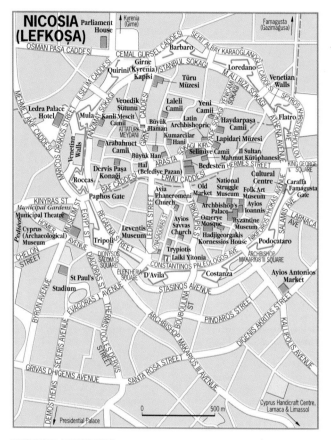

NICOSIA (LEFKOSA)
Parliament House
↑ Kyrenia (Girne)
Famagusta (Gazimağusa) ↑
OSMAN PASA CADDESI
CEMAL GURSEL CADDESI
ŞEHIT ALBAY KARAOĞLANOĞLU CADDESI
Barbaro
Girne
Quirini(Kyrenia) Kapisi
ISTANBUL SOKAĞI
Loredano
Venetian Walls
Türu Müzesi
M ALI RIZA SOKAĞI
SPYROS KYRIAKI...
Ledra Palace Hotel
Venedik Sütunu
Laleli Camii
Yeni Camii
Haydarpaşa Camii
Flatro
Mula
Kanli Mescit Camii
Büyük Haman
Latin Archbishopric
Lapidari Müzesi
ATHENA AVENUE
Arabahmet Camii
ATATURK MEYDANI
Kumarcilar Hani
Selimiye Camii
Il Sultan
KING GEORGE SQUARE
Dervis Paşa Konaği
Büyük Han
AĞI KIRI...
Mahmut Kütüphanesi
Roccas
Hal (Belediye Pazan)
ARASTA
Bedesten
HERMES STREET
Caraffa
Venetian Walls
BAF CADDESI
ERMU CADDESI
National Struggle Museum
Cultural Centre
Famagusta Gate
Paphos Gate
Avia Phaneromeni Church
Old Market
Folk Art Museum
Ayios Ioannis
SALAMIS AVE
KINYRAS ST
Municipal Gardens
Municipal Theatre
TRIKOUPIS STREET
Archbishop's Palace
LARNACA AVE
Cyprus (Archaeological) Museum
Pentico
HOMER
MUSEUM ST
Ayios Savvas Church
Omerye Mosque
Byzantine Museum
NIKIFOROS PHOKAS AVE
EGYPT ST
Leventis Museum
Hadjigeorgakis Kornessios House
Podocataro
Tripoli
REGAENA STREET
ONASSGORS ST
Trypiotis
ARCHBISHOP MAKARIOS III SQUARE
CHELON STREET
AVENUE
DIONYSOS SALOMOS SQUARE
OLIGOROS ST
Laiki Yitonia
DIGENIS AKRITAS STREET
St Paul's
ELEFTHERIA SQUARE
D'Avila
CONSTANTINOS PALEOLOGOS AVE
Costanza
Ayios Antonios Market
Stadium
BYRON AVENUE
EVAGORAS I AVENUE
THERMISTOCLES DERVIS STREET
STASINOS AVENUE
BOUBOULINA ST
ARCHBISHOP MAKARIOS III AVENUE
PINDAROS STREET
KALLIPOLIS AVENUE
SEVERIS AVENUE
GRIVAS DHIGENIS AVENUE
SANTA ROSA STREET
DEMOSTHENIS
Presidential Palace
Cyprus Handicraft Centre, Larnaca & Limassol
0   500 m

NICOSIA (LEFKOSA)

Nicosia (Lefkosa to the Turks), with a population of 171,000, is the capital of the Republic (south Cyprus). It sits on the Mesaoria, or central plain, between two mountain ranges. In summer the plain is an arid dust-bowl, in spring a blaze of colour with wildflowers. This inland siting is unique among the major towns of Cyprus; all the others lie by the shore and suffered terribly at the hands of Arab raiders. Quite simply it became safer to be inland and Nicosia grew out of this reality.

Today, however, Nicosia is a divided city: the 'Green Line' that traverses Cyprus passes through the heart of the old town. No Greeks will be found in the northern section and no Turks in the southern one.

Visitors in the south may gain

limited entry to the north only through the checkpoint at the sandbagged Ledra Palace Hotel, outside the old walls to the west. Visitors from the north cannot visit the south (see page 114). The city of Ottoman grace, domes, minarets and palms has changed dramatically in the last 40 years. It broke free of its ancient and massive walls a long time ago. So today we have two distinct areas, the old and the new. Inside the massive Venetian walls sandstone buildings line the narrow shady streets. The old houses have wooden balconies and peasants walk with baskets of eggs, although not so often these days. In the quieter areas time seems to have stood still, and there is an air of quiet peace, especially early in the morning.

In the Greek sector of the walled city the main shopping area is **Ledra Street** and parallel **Onasagoras Street**. Apart from siesta time these areas are never quiet; shoppers throng the pavements, though some areas have been pedestrianised. Today it is hard to imagine that Ledra Street was once a place to avoid if you valued your life. It was known as 'murder mile' during the EOKA uprising.

Eleftheria (Freedom) **Square** is today the main way through the ancient walls into the old city from the new town. Immediately to the east stands the massive bastion of D'Avila. The square itself spans the dry moat that once protected the city. Nowadays the square is full of activity, with people passing through, waiting for friends, or standing by the typical collection of Cypriot stalls.

Dionysos Salomos Square to the west, by the Tripoli Bastion, is also a cheerful bustling place. Here the reason for congregating is to await the village bus, Cyprus's remarkable and unique specimen of engineering. Between the two squares is **Regaena Street**, known for its fine balconies as well as the seedy bars and nightlife and all that goes with it.

Entry to the Turkish part of the walled city is by **Kyrenia (Girne) Gate**. There is a different air here. Where Greek enterprise has destroyed the past, Turkish inertia, brought on by uncertainty, has preserved it. Buildings have been patched up rather than replaced, shutters and balconies are weathered and bleached, ironwork rusty; mud bricks show where plaster has crumbled and cracked.

The narrow streets rapidly become a maze, with dark tiny shops and stallholders on street corners. Through the decay the remnants of an older Cyprus can be glimpsed, leftovers from the period when Nicosia was the Lusignan capital and Cyprus a Christian kingdom and resting-place for crusaders. The Gothic arches and rose windows of Frankish architecture are seen most clearly in the elevations of the **Selimiye Mosque (Camii)**, previously known as the Cathedral of Santa Sophia, and the **Bedesten** nearby.

Outside the old city, especially in the Greek quarter, it is a different tale. The city has a somewhat prosperous air, gardens are well laid out and looked after.

Archbishop Makarios III Avenue is a wide boulevard of shops and pavement cafés. There is even a Woolworths at the junction with Santa Rosa Street. Traffic rushes around a one-way system, and drivers grow impatient in the heat. Cinemas are popular and some of these are open air. In the west the **Municipal Gardens** are a welcome oasis of trees and flowers.

Across the way, on Museum Street, is the **Municipal Theatre**. There are two or three leisure complexes with swimming pools and tennis courts (see **Sport** page 108). Day members are allowed and visitors staying in the capital at hotels without a pool may find them useful, for in high summer Nicosia is much hotter than the coast. The temperature can go above 38°C (100°F) for days on end.

Life slows down in the back streets

Fortunately, in the late afternoon the cooler air of the mountains alleviates matters. Dusk, which comes about 20.00 hours is a time for barbecues, and all over Nicosia kebabs can be smelled.

History

When the city was founded is not certain, but it seems that after the destruction of Constantia (near Famagusta) on the eastern seaboard in the 7th century, Nicosia grew to become an important centre of administration. It is generally thought that the present city lies close to the ancient settlement of Ledra.

The city flourished and in Lusignan times the royal court was established, resulting in the erection of many fine buildings. Despite the inland position of Nicosia the Mamelukes managed to cross the central plain and sack the town in 1426. After the Venetians had gained control of Cyprus in 1489 they built up the defences of the city. The massive walls and bastions that we see today were started in 1567 and it is ironical that no sooner were the defences complete than the Turks laid siege to the city and in six weeks it had fallen. There was an orgy of slaughter and perhaps 20,000 people were butchered. With the arrival of Ottoman rule the city went rapidly into decline. In 1764 there were riots, leading to the killing of the despotic Turkish governor. Then later, some time in 1821, four bishops and 200 leading Christians were killed by the fanatical governor Kuchuk Mehmed.

Nicosia was partitioned in 1964

The stern figure of ex-president Makarios fronts his Archbishopric

after fighting between Greek and Turkish Cypriots and the United Nations were called in to help keep the peace. Things did not get better and in July 1974, after the overthrow of Makarios by ENOSIS supporters, Turkish mainland forces entered the northern part of the city.

GREEK SECTOR

What to See in the Old City

◆
ARCHBISHOP'S PALACE
Kyprianos Square
It is difficult to miss this ostentatious building of pseudo-Venetian detailing. It was started in 1960 and took many years to construct. In contrast to this extravagance, the bedroom of Archbishop Makarios III, where his heart is preserved, displays only a plain chest and iron bed. The Palace is open to the public only on special occasions (tel: (02) 474411).

◆◆
AYIOS IOANNIS CATHEDRAL (CATHEDRAL OF ST JOHN)
Kyprianos Square
A Benedictine abbey once stood on the site where, it seems, a finger of St John the Baptist was preserved only to be stolen by the Mamelukes in 1426. When the Benedictines left Cyprus the abbey passed into Orthodox hands and in the 1660s the present building was constructed. Some of the old buildings were later renovated and today they house the Folk Art Museum (see opposite). In the early part of the 18th century the walls and vaults of the cathedral were covered with paintings. A *Last Judgement* incorporates a gruesome figure of the 'Ruler of Darkness'. The paintings have recently been restored to their former glory.

◆◆
FAMAGUSTA GATE AND CULTURAL CENTRE
east part of the walled city on Nikiforos Phokas Avenue
Famagusta Gate (or Porta Giuliana) used to be the main entrance to the walled city and is an impressive monument of the Venetian era. It was constructed in 1567 to a military design first used in Crete. The barrel-vaulting has been restored and today the edifice is used as a cultural centre where art exhibitions are held. During the arts festival in September concerts and plays take place close by.
Open: 10.00-13.00 and 16.00-19.00 hrs Monday to Friday, 10.00-13.00 hrs Saturday. Tel: (02) 430877.

◆◆
FOLK ART MUSEUM
Kyprianos Square
The arcaded buildings known as the Old Archbishopric was renovated in 1962-4 to become the museum. Exhibits include a wooden waterwheel, some looms, dowry chests and hand-woven cotton outfits. There are also examples of the famous peasants' baggy pants or *vraka*. Currently closed for renovation. Tel: (02) 463205 for further information.

◆◆
HADJIGEORGAKIS KORNESSIOS HOUSE (KORNAK MANSION)
off Patriarch Gregorio Street
This is one of the best examples of 18th-century Turkish domestic architecture surviving, and is an unusual place, with an overhanging closed balcony. Inside, it is much restored with a painted ceiling and some interesting woodwork. Hadjigeorgakis Kornessios was a dragoman, in fact the Great Dragoman of Cyprus, from 1779-1809. As official interpreter he was held in high esteem and from time to time he would have audience with the Sultan in Constantinople. The restored building houses the Cyprus Ethnographical Museum.
Open: 07.30-13.30 hrs Monday to Saturday in June to September; 07.30-14.00 hrs Monday to Friday and 07.30-13.00 hrs Saturday in October to May.

◆◆
LAIKI YITONIA
Laiki Yitonia (meaning 'local neighbourhood') is an area bordered by Thrace Street and the south end of Trikoupis Street, east of Eleftheria Square. This neighbourhood is a noteworthy attempt to recreate a part, or at least the atmosphere, of old Nicosia. Various buildings have been restored or constructed in traditional Cypriot urban style, and they house a multitude of activities. These include cafés, boutiques, tavernas, galleries and craftsmen's workshops.

◆
OMERYE MOSQUE
Tyllyria Square
Originally the building was the 14th-century Augustinian church of St Mary. In 1571 the victorious Turkish general Mustapha Pasha, believing that the prophet Omer had rested there when visiting Nicosia, raised a minaret and the church was converted into a

mosque. Because of the division of the city, Turks no longer use the mosque. It is, however, used by Arabs who in recent years have come to Nicosia.

◆◆◆
VENETIAN WALLS

These surround the old city and are substantially as constructed in 1567, although crumbling in places. They are a spectacular work but this only becomes evident from the air, when the full encirclement of walls and bastions can be perceived. When the Venetians came to Nicosia the city walls formed a seven-mile (11km) circuit). For strategic reasons they tightened the defensive circle to 2¾ miles (4.5km). Eleven bastions with fine names were incorporated at regular intervals into the design, as were three impressive fortified gates, which we know today as Famagusta Gate, Kyrenia Gate and Paphos Gate. Outside the walls the Venetians dug out a wide moat, merely one more obstacle to an attacker and never intended to carry water.

Famagusta Gate (see page 53), to the east, was the principal entrance to the city and remains the best Venetian monument surviving in Nicosia. The interior of the portal with its large wooden gates is decorated by six coats of arms.

Paphos Gate formed the west entrance to the city. It is now somewhat battered, the proximity of the Green Line ensuring that it was always at the centre of the troubles of recent years.

Kyrenia (Girne) Gate is in the Turkish sector. Traffic does not go through it, but passes on either side. Hence the gate is cut off from the walls, isolated by asphalt.

What to See in the New Town

◆
CYPRUS HANDICRAFT CENTRE

Athalassa Avenue (eastern end)
About 1½ miles (2.3km) to the south of the old city is the Handicraft Centre where people displaced from the north carry out a variety of crafts including weaving, embroidery, wood-carving and pottery. The work areas are set around a quiet courtyard. To find it, turn right at the traffic lights at the start of the Nicosia-Limassol highway.
Open: 07.30-14.30 hrs Monday to Friday also 15.00–18.00 Thursdays; 07.30-13.00 hrs Saturday. Tel: (02) 305024.

◆◆
CYPRUS MUSEUM

Museum Street
Here, a series of 14 rooms takes the visitor through one of the

'Aphrodite' from the Cyprus Museum

best archaeological collections in the Middle East. The exhibits reveal much of the history and cultural development of Cyprus from Neolithic times (6800BC) to the Roman occupation AD300. Items from all over Cyprus are displayed and perhaps the earlier ones are the most spectacular. Of particular interest are the soapstone idols and the red and white pottery from Erimi (3000BC).

Room 4 currently has an exceptional collection of terracotta figures of different sizes. They are part of a discovery of 2,000 votive figurines that were found near Ayia Irini (Akdeniz), north of Morphou (now Güzelyurt). They were lying by the altar of a sanctuary and it is remarkable that only two were female representations.

Noteworthy items include the marble statue of Aphrodite from Soli (1st century BC); a large bronze statue of Septimus Severus, the Roman emperor; the famous conical stone from Palea Paphos (see page 43); some impressive bearded limestone heads; and the head of a woman from Arsos (450-400BC), complete with diadem. *Open:* 09.00–17.00 hrs Monday to Saturday, 10.00-13.00 hrs Sunday. Tel: (02) 30-2189.

◆◆
MUNICIPAL GARDENS
Museum Street
This is a welcome oasis at the rear of the Municipal Theatre. Exhausted sightseers can collapse on to seats located under the palm trees and view the well-tended flower beds.

Accommodation
There are numerous hotels in the city, a few of them actually in the old town. They vary from relatively humble establishments to luxury hotels such as the Hilton and Churchill.

Averof, 19 Averof Street, towards the Green Line west of the old city (tel: (02) 463447 or write to PO Box 4225). A very pleasant traditional hotel of 25 rooms. 2-star.

Cleopatra, 8 Florina Street, central in the new town (tel: (02) 445254 or write to PO Box 1397). A popular 75-room hotel centrally located in the new town. 3-star.

Delphi, 24 Pantelides Avenue, west of Eleftheria Square, old city (tel: (02) 475211). Has 14 adequate rooms with balconies and bathrooms.

Tony's Furnished Flats, 13 Solon Street, old city between Eleftheria Square and Laiki Yitonia (tel: (02) 466752). The management is friendly and there is a roof garden. A traditional English breakfast is available.

Nightlife and Entertainment
The absence of licensing hours means the bars can stay open as long as they want. There are several discothèques and at the weekends these are open into the early hours. The **Crazy Horse Cabaret** is to be found on Homer Avenue; a rival is **Maxim Cabaret** on Princess Zena de Tyra Street. Greek music and pop music nights are a regular feature at **Isadoras** at the junction of Deligeorgis Street and Severis Avenue. Nightclub enthusiasts should try **Casanovas** on

Archbishop Makarios III Avenue or at the **Cleopatra Hotel** in Florina Street.

The Municipal Theatre, in Museum Street puts on regular performances of classical music and plays.

Restaurants

Skorpios, 3 Stassinos Street, Engomi (tel: (02) 445950). First class a la carte and Cypriot cuisine.

Bastioni Café, near Famagusta Gate in old city. Frequented by the beautiful people.

Corona, 15a Orfeos Street, Ayios Dhometios (tel: (02) 444223). Good food in plain surroundings.

Greek Tavern, 46 Griva Dhigenis Avenue (tel: (02) 45555). Greek food, Greek dancing and sometimes Greek plate-smashing.

Navarino, 1 Navarino Street (tel: (02) 450775). A relatively sophisticated place with a very pleasant walled garden interior.

Plaka Taverna, 8 Archbishop Makarios III Square, Engomi. Many excellent local dishes.

Shopping

Virtually anything can be bought in Nicosia. In the new town, Archbishop Makarios III Avenue and adjoining streets are the main shopping thoroughfares. At the north west end of the Avenue is the Capital Centre housing a variety of good quality shops. Ledra Street in the old town is famous for its small shops selling all manner of merchandise. Onasagoras Street, running parallel, is almost as impressive. For local colour visit one of the open-air markets. The Old Market is off Trikoupis Street in the old town, and market days are Friday and Saturday.

TURKISH SECTOR

The best way into the old city is through **Kyrenia (Girne) Gate** and along Girne Caddesi to Atatürk Meydani with its interesting buildings from colonial days. In the centre of the roundabout is a **Venetian Column** of grey granite brought initially from the ruins of Salamis to the Sarayönü Mosque in the 15th century. It was placed in its present position in 1915. Once, the 20-feet (6m) high column carried a lion of St Mark. This was lost and replaced by a copper dome by the British. The fountain to the north of the square is of the Ottoman period.

What to See in the Old City

For opening times of museums etc, see **Directory** page 117.

◆
ARABAHMET CAMII
Mufti Ziyai Effendi Sokagi
Built in 1845, the mosque claims to preserve part of the Prophet's beard, or at least one hair from it, this being shown to the Faithful once a year. The mosque is one of the most beautiful of the Ottoman era. A fountain and tombs can be seen in the courtyard.

◆
BEDESTAN
Arasta Sokagi
In Venetian times it was a Greek Orthodox cathedral and survived as such until the Turkish conquest in 1571, when it suffered relegation to a grain store. Above the impressive

north door are six Venetian coats of arms and in the highest part of the gable a delicate tracery is to be seen.

◆◆
BÜYÜK HAMAN
Mousa Orfenbey Sokagi
Originally the church of St George of the Latins (14th century), this was later converted to Turkish baths. Of the church only the entrance remains. On the west side is a small café whose proprietor will open the building on request.

◆◆
BÜYÜK KHAIN (HAN)
Arasta Sokagi
The 'Han' is an impressive building being extensively refurbished, and when finished it will be a museum. First built as an inn in 1572, it became Nicosia's central prison in 1893. It is open to the public from time to time.

◆◆
DERVIS PASA KONAGI (DERVISH PASHA'S MANSION)
Belig Pasa Sokagi in the Arabahmet quarter
The building dates from 1807. Dervish Pasha was the owner and editor of the first Turkish newspaper in Cyprus. There are two floors: the lower level was used as a store and for servants,

Büyük Khain (Han)

the upper floor for the family. Restoration work was completed in 1988.

Now it is a museum of ethnography, one part being arranged as a bedroom, dining room, bride's room and weaving room. The other part is set out as a living room. There is a courtyard complete with flower beds and a pomegranate tree.

◆
LAPIDARI MUZESI (MUSEUM)
Zuhtizade Sokagi

The museum houses a display of stone relics from the Selimiye Mosque and various other holy places. The building itself is a 15th-century Venetian house. Access is by courtesy of the custodian of the Library of Sultan Mohamed II, across the way by the Selimiye Mosque.

◆◆◆
TÜRK MUZESI (TURKISH MUSEUM)
Girne Caddesi by Girne Gate

This was once the home of the Dervish sect of the Mevlevi

Selimiye Mosque, once a cathedral

religious order, famous for its characteristic whirling dance. The building was constructed in the 17th century and is now a museum for Turkish arts and crafts. Musical instruments, costumes, embroidery, glass and metalwork are kept around a wooden floor. A musicians' gallery looks down on where the Dervishes once whirled. Adjoining the museum is a mausoleum containing a long line of tombs, among them that of Selim Dede, the last Sheikh of the city.

◆◆◆
SELIMIYE CAMII

Selimiye Sokagi

The mosque is the most important medieval building in Nicosia. Before 1954 it was known as the **Cathedral of Santa Sophia**, the name being changed in honour of Sultan Selim II in whose reign the Turks captured the island.

The building inside and out has a neglected look about it; nevertheless, it is an impressive work of French Gothic architecture. Construction of the cathedral was started by the Lusignans in 1209 and even when the building was consecrated in 1326 some work was still unfinished. It suffered damage at the hands of the Genoese in 1375 and again by the Mamelukes some 50 years later. In the 16th century it was converted into a mosque and all Christian features removed with the exception of various tombstones which were used to pave the floor. Some time later the twin minarets were added. The work of French craftsmen is especially fine in the porch and the great west window. Visitors may enter (skirts are available for those clad in shorts), and on passing through the narthex entrance area will find a whitewashed Gothic nave of five bays supported by massive pillars and a semicircular apse. Above the north transept is the Women's Gallery with a small chapel close by.

VENETIAN WALLS
See page 54.

In the **New Town** to the northwest in the Kumsal area is the **Museum of Barbarism**. The exhibits, which relate to the inter-communal troubles during and after 1963, are found in the house of Major Ilhan, a Turkish army doctor whose wife and children were killed by EOKA terrorists. It is open during office hours.

Accommodation

Sabri's Orient, Old City (tel: (020) 72162). 38-room hotel outside the city ramparts on the main road to Kyrenia (Girne). 1-star.

Saray Hotel, Atatürk Meydani (tel: (020) 83115). Turkish Nicosia's leading hotel with 74 rooms. 3-star.

Restaurants

Exhausted midday sightseers can get their lunch on the lower level of the modern shopping arcade called **Galleria**, southwest of the Selimiye Mosque where the waiters speak some English.

For the evening, **Anibal** restaurant at the east end of the Green Line by Famagusta Gate is a place for *meze* and *kebab*.

The food of the **Saray Roof** restaurant in Atatürk Meydani (tel: (020) 83115) is perhaps inferior, but the view is excellent. Many local people make the four-mile (6.5km) trip to the **Hanedan**, on the road to Güzelyurt. The proprietor developed his culinary skills in Australia.

Shopping

In many respects time has stood still in the old city. Shops selling onyx, copper items, ceramics and silver jewellery are as they were years ago. It is possible to get leather shoes made to measure in 24 hours. There are numerous tailors' shops well stocked with high quality dress and suit material. The one modern area is called the **Galleria**: it is on two levels and for some reason has a preponderance of sports shops.

Next to the Bedestan is the **market**, a place to get fresh fruit and vegetables.

THE HIGH TROODOS

◆◆◆
ASINOU CHURCH (PANAYIA PHORVIOTISSA)

25 miles (40km) southwest of Nicosia

Asinou is in the foothills of the Troodos Mountains. From Nicosia take the road to Troodos and then south to Vizakia after approximately 20 miles (32km). The priest with the key is found at Nikitari, the next village (3 miles/5km away), he will accompany visitors to the church.

This charming little place sits on a lovely wooded hillside. Visitors will be surprised to find a steep double pitched roof on such an old building. However, this roof is merely an outer covering to the domes and barrel vaults below and is typical of Cypriot churches.

The church was built in 1105 and the dome to the narthex (entrance area) was added in 1200. One hundred years later the barrel vault was remade and the nave buttressed.

Asinou is the best of Cyprus's painted churches. The frescos covering the dome of the narthex and the walls of the apse and nave are a fascinating record of Byzantine and Post-Byzantine art from the time the church was built to the 16th century.

◆
AYIOS IRAKLIDHIOS MONASTERY

12 miles (19km) southwest of Nicosia

The monastery lies a little beyond the village of Politiko in fine country. It was founded in Byzantine times, but the present buildings date from 1759. A community of nuns lives here today and they find time to tend the pleasing gardens as well as sell almond honey and other confections.

◆◆◆
KAKOPETRIA

35 miles (50km) southwest of Nicosia

The village lies in a poplar-filled valley halfway up the north slope of Mount Olympus at a height of 2,200 feet (670m). Like most Cypriot hill villages, Kakopetria has a decrepit air. This is part of its charm and artists especially seem to find such ramshackle places an inspiration. The village's old quarter is a protected area and some of its old buildings have been restored.

Kakopetria has a few small hotels and some restaurants. In summer it is a busy resort and the population of about 1,300 trebles with the influx of Cypriots from the hot lowlands.

Above the village is the Byzantine church of **Ayios Nikolaos tis Steyis** (St Nicholas of the Roof). It is an unusual building from the outside, mainly because of the huge shingle roof that protects the lower domed and tiled roof. The original building is of the 11th century with 12th-century additions. Inside is a wealth of frescos, many painted at the time the church was built, some as late as the 17th century. The *Nativity* is of the 14th century, the *Transfiguration* much earlier. As

the church is usually locked it is essential to ask for the whereabouts of the key in Kakopetria.

◆◆◆
KYKKO MONASTERY ✓

western Troodos (12½ miles (20km) west of Pedhoulas village)
The monastery is fairly remote, although today it can be reached from the east on metalled roads. It is the richest and most renowned in Cyprus and known throughout the Orthodox world. It stands among pine forests at a height of 3,800 feet (1,160m) above sea-level, pleasantly cool in summer, but too cold in winter. Kykko owes its foundation and fame to the gift of an icon of the Virgin Mary in the 12th century. This is attributed to the hand of St Luke, one of only three such works in existence. Unfortunately for the visitor it has for centuries been considered too sacred to gaze upon, and is suitably concealed by a silver plate embossed with a picture of

High in the hills, Kykko Monastery is a cool retreat from Nicosia's heat

the portrait behind. The rain-making powers of the icon are called upon by the monks and local people when necessary. A hermit named Isaiah founded the monastery in 1100, having been given the precious icon for curing Emperor Alexios Comnenos' daughter of sciatica. The building was burnt down in 1365, 1542, 1751 and 1831, the icon miraculously surviving each fiery disaster.
Visitors are welcome to stay and rooms are provided for them. At weekends it can be a busy place. On a hill called **Throni** (two miles/3km west) overlooking the monastery to the west is the burial place of President Makarios (Archbishop Makarios III). The views are superb from here.

◆◆
MAKHERAS MONASTERY
eastern Troodos
The monastery lies 25½ miles (41km) to the southwest of

THE HIGH TROODOS

Nicosia, through Deftera and Pera villages. Visitors from Limassol should first proceed east to connect up with the Larnaca route.

The monastery was founded in 1148 by two monks. The small community extended the accommodation and in 1172 it gained its first abbot. In 1530 the building was burnt down, and suffered the same fate in 1892. When rebuilding was carried out little from the past was retained. Although the monastery has no great architectural merit, the drive through the wooded hillsides, climbing to a height of 2,890 feet (880m) above sea-level, makes it all worth while.

Moutoullas, famed for its spring water, is a typical Troodos mountain village, precariously perched on the steep hillside

◆◆
PANAYIA TOU ARAKA (LAGOUDHERA CHURCH)
central Troodos, off the Kakopetria-Troodos-Limassol road, Lagoudhera village
The church is a single-aisled vaulted building with three arched recesses in each of the side walls and a dome over the centre, typical of the mid-Byzantine period. This entire structure is covered with a protective steep-pitched tiled roof which also covers a later enclosure built in timber. It dates from 1192 although the tiled roof was replaced in the 18th century. Inside is a complete series of wall paintings, some of the best in the island. From the dome, *Christ Pantocrator*, Ruler of the World, looks down; the *Presentation of the Virgin Mary* is given prominence in the north

arched recess. Visitors can obtain the key from the priest, who lives next door to the church.

◆◆
PERISTERONA CHURCH (AYII VARNAVA AND HILARION)
17 miles (27km) west of Nicosia
Reached on the Nicosia-Troodos road, the church stands by the boulder-strewn Peristerona river, the bed of which is dry in summer and a torrent in winter. Its five domes are rivalled in Cyprus only by the church at Yeroskipou (see page 41). It dates from the early 10th century and is dedicated to Saints Barnabas and Hilarion.

◆◆
SCENIC ROUTE INTO TROODOS
Anybody with the time should take the scenic route up (or down) the north flank of Mount Olympus. The road twists and turns and there are a few dramatic hairpin bends giving some fine views. Each village in turn spills down the hillside, a collection of solid buildings and dilapidated shacks.
Kalopanayiotis, the lowest village has some sulphur springs and a dam. Near by is the monastery of **Ayios Ioannis Lampadistis** with a church dating from the 11th century. Within are some excellent frescos of the 13th and 15th centuries.
Moutoullas is famous for its spring water, bottles of which are sent all over the island. A little further up the mountain, cherry orchards adorn the slopes around **Pedhoulas,** a

The Byzantine splendour of a chandelier in the ancient church of Ayii Varnava and Hilarion

spectacular sight in springtime. **Prodhromos** at 4,560 feet (1,390m) above sea-level is the highest true village of Cyprus. The scenic route is approached from the north by taking the road to Throni, four miles (6.5km) after the road junction to Koutraphas and before the climb up the mountain.

◆
STAVROS TOU AYIASMATI (CHURCH OF THE HOLY CROSS)
central Troodos, just under 2 miles (3km) northwest of Platanistassa
The church lies in a fold in the northern slopes of the remote hills. It has an almost complete series of wall paintings of the 15th century, the finest in Cyprus. They include *The Last*

THE HIGH TROODOS

The church in Pedhoulas village is dedicated to the Archangel Michael

Supper, The Washing of the Feet and *The Betrayal*. Enquire for the key at Platanistassa.

◆
TAMASSUS
12 miles (19km) southwest of Nicosia
The site is in lovely country, immediately northeast of the village of Politiko. Not a great deal remains to be seen today. Tamassus, one of the oldest city kingdoms, was made rich by copper discovered in 2500BC, and perhaps the city really is the 'Temese' mentioned in the Odyssey as is often suggested. *Open:* 09.00-12.00 and 16.00-19.00 hrs Tuesday to Sunday in June to September; 09.00-13.00 and 14.00-16.30 hrs rest of year.

Accommodation
The hotels in the hill resorts are of a good standard with a range of facilities, some with swimming pools. For the more adventurous there are youth hostels and camping sites.
Churchill Pinewood Valley, Pedhoulas village (tel: (02) 952211). 33 rooms in a pleasant setting. 3-star.
Forest Park, Platres village (tel: (05) 421751). The hotel has 80 rooms and is pleasantly placed among pine trees. Has a swimming pool. 4-star.
Hekali, Kakopetria village (tel: (02) 922501). A modest establishment with modest prices. 30 rooms. 2-star.
Jack's, Pedhoulas village (tel: (02) 952350). A small family-run hotel with 20 rooms. 1-star.
Kifissia, Kakopetria village (tel: (02) 922421). Good double rooms overlooking a stream. English breakfast provided. 43 rooms. 1-star.
Troodos Hotel, Troodos village (tel: (05) 421635). A family-run business with 49 rooms. Hot stoves in winter. 3-star.

KYRENIA, GÜZELYURT AND ON TO KANTARA

This section takes in the great sweep of Güzelyurt Körfezi (Morphou Bay) from Erenköy to Koruçam Burnu (Cape Kormakiti) and the whole of the Kyrenia hills.

The latter are an impressive backbone of rock which runs unbroken for 50 miles (80km) along the northern coast, a dramatic background to the villages among the olive groves of the coastal strip. Griffon vultures soar in formation among rocky crags. **Buffavento Castle** rears majestically above **Bellapais Abbey**, and **St Hilarion Castle** looks down on Kyrenia from its impregnable eyrie.

Out in the east the third of the great Lusignan Castles, **Kantara**, has a similar magical setting, but now the spectacular chain of high ground falls gradually into the low-lying terrain of the Karpas peninsula (an area covered in the next chapter). Kyrenia (Girne) is the only place of any size on the northern littoral and it has the only harbour of any consequence. Across the sea on a clear day the mountains of Turkey are plainly visible.

Over in the west the sandy beaches of Güzelyurt Körfezi circle round to where the foothills of the western Troodos reach out for the shore. Here by the sea can be found the ancient palace of **Vouni** and a little inland the site of **Soli** and its Roman theatre.

Güzelyurt is the centre of a rich agricultural region, the production of citrus fruits and strawberries and vegetables being made possible by extensive irrigation.

The expanse of Güzelyurt Bay is one of the sights of Cyprus's north coast

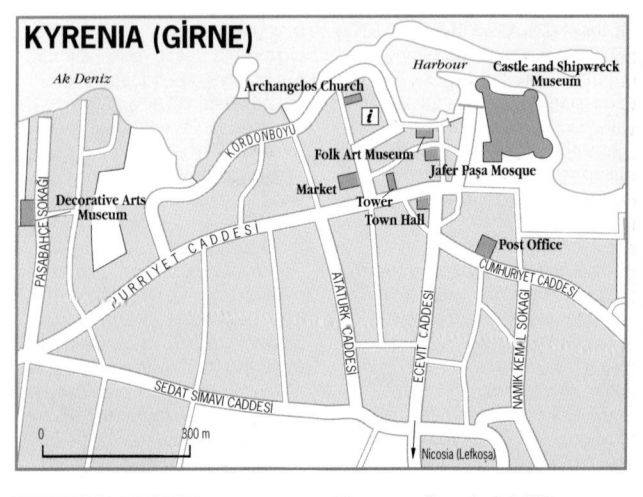

KYRENIA (GİRNE)

Ak Deniz

KORDONBOYU

Archangelos Church

Harbour Castle and Shipwreck Museum

Folk Art Museum

Jafer Paşa Mosque

Market

Tower
Town Hall

Decorative Arts Museum

PAŞABAHÇE SOKAĞI

HÜRRIYET CADDESI

ATATÜRK CADDESI

SEDAT SIMAVI CADDESI

ECEVIT CADDESI

Post Office

CUMHURIYET CADDESI

NAMIK KEMAL SOKAĞI

0   300 m

Nicosia (Lefkoşa)

KYRENIA (GIRNE)

Kyrenia is a charming place. The Venetian mansions that line the horseshoe-shaped harbour have been turned into cafés and restaurants and one can sit under the coloured umbrellas and gaze over the boats lying at anchor to the massive ramparts of Kyrenia castle, which pushes a huge cylindrical bastion out into the harbour. Add to this a few palm trees, minarets and the magnificent backcloth of the Kyrenia hills and you have a holiday town that for once lives up to the descriptions of the tourist literature.

Nevertheless, the rest of the town is not quite up to the standard of the harbour area, and a drawback is the beach, or lack of one, for the shore is somewhat rocky. However, sun-worshippers and swimmers will find sandy shores a few miles to the east or west (see page 74).

The town, founded 3,000 years ago by the Achaeans, was part of the ancient city-kingdom of Kyrenia. Under the Romans it became Corineum. To the south the town was well protected by the Kyrenia hills, but there was no such security to the north and it suffered periodically at the hands of raiders. As a result defensive walls and towers were built and improved upon over the years. A fort was constructed by the Byzantines and extended in the early 13th century by the Lusignan king Hugh I. These fortifications helped Kyrenia to survive centuries of piracy and some of the remains of the towers can be seen today. There is one down by the harbour and a larger and better preserved example at the junction of Attila Sokagi and Hürriyet Caddesi (near the market). In 1374 the garrison withstood a fearful onslaught by the Genoese, overturning siege towers and hurling rocks from the battlements. Nevertheless, when the Venetians subjugated Cyprus they were not satisfied with Kyrenia's defences and, using their considerable skills in military architecture, constructed the castle we see today.

As with Nicosia the defences proved to be of no avail when the Ottoman Turks came in 1570. In fact, Kyrenia surrendered with hardly a shot being fired. The port was renamed Gerinia, not so much different from the Turkish name 'Girne' used today.

A century after the Ottoman takeover Kyrenia was described by an eminent traveller as 'ruinous'. By the beginning of the 19th century only a handful of families lived there. However, after the arrival of the British in 1878, communications with Nicosia were improved and the population increased. At this time the harbour facilities were enhanced and breakwaters constructed. British colonial officials took a liking to Kyrenia and it became a place of retirement where they led a life according to Lawrence Durrell, himself a resident of nearby Bellabayis (Bellapais), of 'blameless monotony'.

During the troubles of 1974 Turkish forces landed to the west of Kyrenia. The Greek Cypriots fled and the British left, although many of the latter were to return. A new port has been built east of the harbour and these days a hydrofoil service connects Kyrenia with Turkey.

The harbour at Kyrenia (Girne)

WHAT TO SEE

For opening hours see **Directory** pages 117–18.

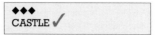

**◆◆◆
CASTLE** ✓

by the harbour
Lusignan kings regularly stayed in the castle, the origins of which go back to Byzantine times. Much later, during the British occupation, the castle was used as a prison. But eventually it became the responsibility of the Department of Antiquities who saw it much restored in 1955. Entry is by a modern bridge. A narrow passage leads to a 12th-century Byzantine chapel and then turns back to the massive northwest tower. An alternative route is to continue straight on through the gatehouse and into the main courtyard where lies the tomb of Sadik Pasha, the Turkish naval commander killed in the conquest of 1570. From the northwest tower the battlements can be gained, where the views of the mountains are fantastic and the

unguarded drop from the walls quite dangerous.

On the east side of the main courtyard is a unique exhibition in the **Shipwreck Museum**. From an air-conditioned viewing gallery one can see the famous **Kyrenia Ship**, wrecked in 300BC in relatively shallow waters close to Kyrenia. The remarkable discovery was made by a Cypriot diver during a routine exploration. Lifting the wreck from the seabed was a delicate task but one that was successfully carried out in 1969 by the University of Pennsylvania. It is the oldest vessel ever to be recovered from the sea. Another six years passed before the assembly of the hull, fittings and cargo of plates and amphorae was complete.

Access to the royal apartments is across the courtyard to the west, although few rooms remain. Dungeons carved out of rock can be found below.

To reach the southwest tower one must return to the battlements. A little beyond the tower is a passage down into the southwest bastion. From here a walk along the west wall leads to a stair and down to the entrance to complete the tour.

◆

DECORATIVE ARTS MUSEUM
Pasabahçe Sokagi

The museum exhibits oil paintings, handicrafts from the Far East and European and Chinese porcelain.

◆

FOLK ART MUSEUM
by the harbour

Various hand-made objects, pieces of furniture of the 18th century and the implements used to make them are displayed. The building itself is a model of a Greek Cypriot house of the 18th century.

Accommodation

There are several hotels of varying categories in Kyrenia. Here are a few:

Anadol, Hürriyet Caddesi (tel: (081) 52319). Centrally located with 22 rooms. 2-star.

Bristol, Hürriyet Caddesi (tel: (081) 52298). Centrally located, low-cost with 12 rooms. 1-star.

Dorana, (tel: (081) 53521). West of the harbour, near-central position. 30 rooms. 3-star.

There are other places to stay – mainly self-catering – a few miles from Kyrenia, including:

Ambelia Village, 4 miles (6.5km) south (tel: (081) 52175). 18 studios and 32 villas with a lovely setting high in the pine-clad Kyrenia Hills. It has a small pool and bar restaurant. Not at

Kyrenia's castle, as seen today, is the work of Venetian builders

all suitable for the old or infirm.
Celebrity Bungalows, at Lapta,
9¼ miles (15km) west (tel:
(0821) 8751). A superb oasis of
33 bungalows and 2 luxury villas
set around a pool.
Club Acapulco, 5½ miles (9km)
east (tel: (084) 14110). 60
bungalows overlooking the sea.
It has a restaurant, self service
and taverna with live music.
Club Kyrenia Hotel (tel: (081)
54801). 64 rooms. A new and
prestigious hotel 2 miles (3km)
east of Kyrenia. 3-star.
Courtyard Inn, Karakum 2 miles
(3km) east (tel: (081) 53343).
For those on a limited budget.

Nightlife

Kyrenia is not a place that
comes alive in the early hours.
However, the bars around the
harbour will serve drinks as
long as they have customers.
The hotel **Liman** near the church
of Archangelos not far from the
harbour, runs a casino and so
does the **Dome Hotel**. A
number of hotels, including the
Dome, have discothèques.

Restaurants

If the harbour area of Kyrenia
had been designed by
restaurateurs it could not be
better for eating out. Virtually all
the buildings on the quayside
house restaurants and cafés of
one sort or another. In the
daylight it is a memorable
experience to sit at the tables by
the water's edge, and in the
evening, when all is lit up, it is
even better. One would
normally expect to pay
handsomely for this privilege,
but once the shock of seeing the
prices in thousands *(lira)* has

passed off, it becomes clear that
the meals are not expensive.
It seems almost unjust to single
out particular establishments but
here are a few pointers. The
Harbour Club (tel: (081) 52211)
serves French cuisine upstairs;
down on the pavement there is
different fare and 15 types of
meze can be taken before
moving on to the main course. A
little further around the harbour
is the **Marabou** (tel: (081)
52292). Here the steaks are
mouth-watering and the apple
pie a delight.
Continuing along the waterfront
there are two fish restaurants
with splendid elevated
positions, a Pizza House, and
eventually the famous **Halil's**
where diners see how things
are done Turkish style.
Astonishingly, it is possible to
get bored with the exquisite
harbour and this calls for a visit
to the walled garden of the
Ristorante Italiano (tel: (081)
56845) on the first back street
by the mosque.
A little to the west of the Dome
Hotel is **Niazi's**, famous for its
kebabs. Nevertheless, the
steaks rival those of the
Marabou; other dishes are also
excellent and the fresh fruit an
extravagance. An electric organ
provides background music.
The **Altinkaya** (tel: (082) 18341)
claims to be the most popular
fish restaurant in north Cyprus.
This is situated five miles (8km)
from Kyrenia, on the road going
west to Lapta.
And at Bellabayis is the **Abbey
House Restaurant** (tel: (081)
53460) serving some of the
finest continental cuisine.
Advance booking is advisable.

FROM GÜZELYURT KÖRFEZI TO KANTARA

For opening times of museums, etc see **Directory** pages 117–18.

◆◆

ANTIPHONITIS

18 miles (29km) east of Kyrenia
A track from the village of Bahçeli brings one into a hidden valley and on to the 12th-century church of Antiphonitis. Four columns and four piers rise from an octagonal plan to support a large dome. The narthex (entrance area) was added in the 14th century and the well proportioned loggia in the 15th century. Wall paintings once covered much of the interior. Village boys will insist on being guides from Bahçeli. The easier way to the church is via Esentepe, where a passable road brings one near to the complex.

◆

AYIOS MAMAS MONASTERY

Güzelyurt
Güzelyurt, known as Morphou pre-1974, is a sizeable town and its streets are an incredible maze. Visitors from Kyrenia (Girne) should follow the Lefke signs until they reach the town square where they should see the monastery, or a modern mosque or the police station. The monastery dates from the Byzantine era although much rebuilding took place in the 15th century. Some of this survives despite further alterations in two separate periods in the 18th century. The central dome was added on the first of these occasions. An iconostasis embraces various styles and the

lower panels are exceedingly important examples of Venetian work. The tomb of Ayios Mamas is found in a recess on the north side of the church.

Access is by courtesy of the custodian of the **Museum of Archaeology and Natural History** next door. This museum displays relics of the Late Cypriot age.

◆◆◆

BELLAPAIS ABBEY

4 miles (6.5km) southeast of Kyrenia
Overlooking the sea from an escarpment by the village of Bellabayis, on the lower slopes of the Kyrenian hills, the abbey is an important work of Gothic architecture. It was founded around 1200 as a house of Augustinian canons by Aimery de Lusignan.

The main entrance is from the southwest through an arched gateway. At the other side of the forecourt is a 13th-century church, the earliest surviving part of the abbey. Apart from the iconostasis the interior is Frankish Gothic, with a nave and two aisles, a north and south transept and a chancel. A night stair climbs up to a dormitory. To the west a spiral stair gives access to the roof and a splendid view over the abbey and the mountains. Returning to the forecourt one finds a doorway that leads to the centrepiece of Bellapais, the **cloister**, complete with tall cypress trees. Although it is dilapidated, it is an impressive place with fine Gothic details. The custodian does not normally invite visitors to look at the

Bellapais Abbey, a Gothic jewel

interior of the abbey, but may do so on request.

Adjacent to the abbey is the **Tree of Idleness** made famous by Lawrence Durrell in his book *Bitter Lemons*. It is a good place to sit and rest a while.

◆
BUFFAVENTO CASTLE
8 miles (13km) southeast of Kyrenia

The castle stands high in the hills; the most direct route is via Ayios Khrysostomos Monastery (blocked by the military). An approach from the east is possible. This is from the high point of the pass on the flanks of Pentadaktylos Mountain (Besparmark). Cars should be left in the parking area from where the walk is about 2½ miles (4km).

This is not the best preserved of the three great castles that used to stand guard in the northern mountains, but at nearly 2,600 feet (790m) above the sea it is the highest. Far below, the village of Çatalköy sits among the olive and almond trees of the coastal plain and distant Kyrenia shimmers on a hazy shore.

The three castles formed a chain of communication using flares at night. During the winter months the cold Anatolian wind can blow, a sharp reminder that the name of the castle means 'blown by the wind'. Not much is known of the castle's detailed history but it certainly existed in the 12th century. A garrison was in occupation until well into the Venetian period but, ironically, the last few years of this foreign domination saw the castle dismantled and left to the elements.

◆◆◆
KANTARA CASTLE
2½ miles (4km) north of Kantara Village

Reached along a metalled road, the castle stands over 2,000 feet (630m) above sea-level on the eastern extremity of the jagged Kyrenia hills. The panorama is spectacular. To the south is the great sweep of Gazimagusa Körfezi (Famagusta Bay) and to the north the Taurus Mountains of Turkey. Way below, the Karpas peninsula points to the distant but invisible shore of Syria and, once in a lifetime perhaps, one might see the mountains of Lebanon.

Lofty Kantara Castle

The castle was the last link in the chain of Byzantine coastal defences. Later, along with its neighbours Buffavento and St Hilarion, it was refurbished by the Lusignans and during the Genoese occupation became an inaccessible citadel of resistance. Nevertheless, it ultimately suffered the same fate as the others when it was dismantled by the Venetians in the early part of the 16th century.

Much of the interior is a ruin but the formidable outer wall is mainly intact. Entrance is gained through a ruined barbican by

twin towers, followed by a climb up steps to a vaulted room.

◆◆◆
SAINT HILARION CASTLE ✓

The castle stands on the heights above Kyrenia. The road to the impressive fortifications turns off the Nicosia-Kyrenia highway where it starts its long descent to the coast. It is clearly signposted.

In common with Buffavento and Kantara castles, the lofty site was chosen to give early warning of invaders from the northern seas and the central plain. From this magnificent eyrie at 2,400 feet (732m) the fall of the land to the coastal strip is especially spectacular.

The name of the castle is attributed to a hermit called Hilarion from the Holy Land who lived on the site some time in the 10th or 11th century in a small monastery. After Cyprus was passed to the Lusignans, they promptly strengthened the castle in line with their policy of making the island impregnable. The castle was further improved in the 14th century. In these unusually tranquil times it was frequently used as a summer residence by the Lusignan court. Inevitably all this ended when the Genoese, seeking control of the island, laid siege to the castle. With the arrival of the Venetians in 1489 the nature of warfare changed and the castle's importance was much diminished. The buildings were neglected and a period of decay started that was never arrested. Even so, the castle is the best preserved of the three great castles of the northern mountains.

Once through the entrance the visitor will see a restored gatehouse and on the left a barbican. Here the **lower ward** once housed a garrison and their mounts. By the south wall is a cistern and further on the stables. An ascent to the next level brings some fine views of the walls and a semi-circular tower. From this position one enters the **middle ward** to reach the 10th-century Byzantine church at the top of the stairs, partially restored but missing its dome. Accommodation to the northeast was for the royal family. Today this is a restaurant from where the prospect over the coast is excellent.

Visitors often fail to realise that the **upper ward** is a separate entity reached by a path that commences at the northwestern end of the middle ward. It is a stiff climb to the highest level. At a good height an ascent to the left of the main route leads to St John's Tower. Trees and shrubs cling to the rocky crag which is sheer on three sides. The main path continues to the top. Paths and steps wind past a cistern and on through an arched gateway. To the right are the remains of the kitchens and to the west the ruins of royal apartments. The Queen's window has side seats and although it has lost much of its tracery it retains a view that is surely still as splendid as it must have been in those far-off days. This is as high as one can sensibly proceed. It is a good place to linger a while.

◆◆
SOLI
southern shore of Güzelyurt Körfezi

The city was founded at the beginning of the 6th century BC and became one of the 10 city kingdoms of Cyprus. Like Vouni, just to the west, it played a leading role in the struggle against the Persians. In Roman times it was a centre for copper exports, but following frequent Arab raids in the 7th century, it was destroyed.

The **theatre**, built in the 2nd century AD, is the main feature of the site and was carved out of the hillside overlooking the sea. Lower down the hill are the remains of the **basilica**. Here part of the mosaic floor is in a good state of preservation; the bird designs are most remarkable. Over at the west of the site is the **agora**.

◆◆◆
VOUNI
south of Güzelyurt Körfezi

About 5½ miles (9km) west of Gemikonagi the steep road turns towards the sea and approaches a plateau which is the site of the palace at 910 feet (277m) and gives spectacular views over the bay.

The site was excavated in 1928-9 and, as nothing earlier than the 5th century BC was unearthed, it has been claimed that it is not Vouni at all. Some evidence suggests that the palace was built by a pro-Persian king at the time Salamis was in unsuccessful revolt against the Persians (see page 82–3). Other factors indicate that the palace was constructed in the aftermath of a later revolt when a pro-Greek dynasty was set up. Whatever the truth, it is certain that the palace was set alight and destroyed in 380BC when the Persians regained control. Little remains of the original walls built in the form of three terraces, although the lowest levels have been reset in concrete. It seems clear, however, that there were several different and distinct periods of building.

Beaches

Finding the beaches on the northern shore is a little bit of a struggle although the scenery is marvellous. There are no long expanses of sand and much of the coast is rocky or stony and some of it strewn with rubbish. Kyrenia itself has no beach although the east side of the castle flanks a little cove.

Three miles (5km) to the east of Kyrenia on the road to Esentepe is **Karakum** beach. Further on is **Acapulco** beach, a small bay worth a visit. The sand shelves gently into the sea and it is a good place for swimming. All around are holiday villas, and semi-permanent sunshades have been constructed across the sands.

A further 2½ miles (3.5km) on is **Lara** beach, small but sandy in parts and with some unusual rock formations. There are some changing cabins and a café. The coastal drive is splendid and about 13 miles (21km) out from Kyrenia the shore becomes a series of sand dunes. A track by one of the many small bridges leads to a quiet beach with another a short distance to the west. This is isolated territory and 7½ miles (12km) after the turn to Esentepe one unexpectedly comes across a delightful little cove with two large palm trees. The coast road in varying states of repair continues on to Kaplica, soon after which it turns inland. There are a few interesting coves on this stretch and a beach just east of Kaplica. A few miles west of Kyronia is **Riviera Mocamp**, a rocky place with a few sandy stretches and some holiday development. Further on is the hotel **Deniz Kizi** and here there is a good sandy beach, although dominated by the hotel. Overlooking the beaches from the hillside is the village of Lapta (Lapithos) famous for its lemon groves. There are some interesting old houses here and a perpetual spring.

Thereafter the shoreline runs relatively unspoilt to Güzelyali where the road turns off to Güzelyurt. Here there is a long stretch of shingle overlooked by the wild peaks of the Kyrenia hills. Along the narrow but reasonable road to Kayalar a variety of small shingly inlets can be seen.

Güzelyurt Körfezi forms the western boundary of this section and is bordered in many places by long stretches of sand. It is off the tourist track and there are few facilities.

Accommodation

There is no accommodation for visitors on the west coast except the 1-star **Güzelyurt Hotel** which has 14 rooms (tel: (071) 43412).

A corner of the old fortified city of Famagusta (Gazimagusa)

FAMAGUSTA, THE MESAORIA AND THE KARPAS

This section covers most of eastern Cyprus. The Mesaoria is the Greek name for the flat central plain, the Karpas (known by the Turks as Kirpasa) is a narrow finger of land running east. Both these areas and Famagusta fall within the Turkish-controlled zone. Our southern boundary is the Green Line where it runs from Famagusta to skirt the British Sovereign Base of Dekhelia before looping northwest to Nicosia (Lefkosa).

Old Famagusta is a walled city as impressive as Jerusalem and more complete than Istanbul or Antioch. The new town to the south, called Varosha, is an expanse of hotels and flats, built in the late 1960s and 1970s. Much of its lines the sandy shore. Varosha is many times the size of the old city and today it is forbidden territory, closed to civilians by the Turks. The old town can however be visited. To the west of Famagusta is the flat emptiness of the Mesaoria, a desert in summer, much given to minor whirlwinds and once crossed by camel trains. This dry-season wilderness always had a neglected air and now it seems even more so. As with the rest of Cyprus, the land is transformed in the spring by a blaze of wildflowers.

The ruins of ancient **Salamis** lie by the shore about six miles (9.5km) north of Famagusta. Here there are archaeological discoveries more impressive than any others in Cyprus,

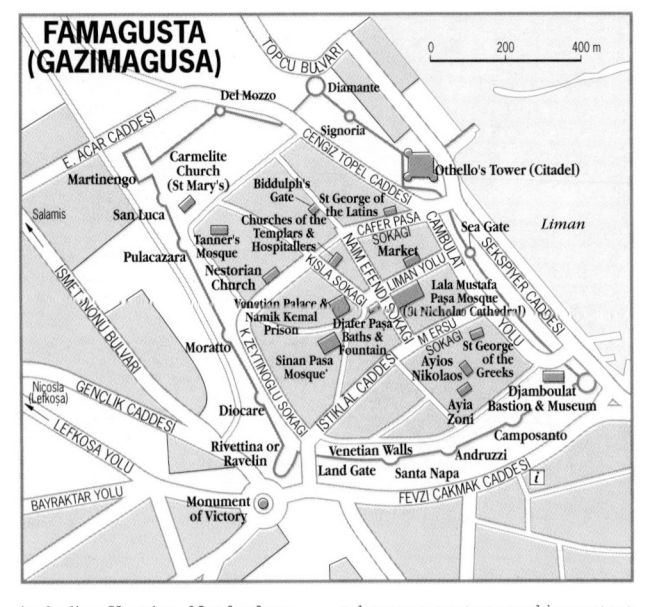

including Kourion. Not far from
the ruins is the **Monastery of
Apostolos Varnavas**, a
Christian church now in Muslim
territory. At the northern
extremity of Gazimaguza
Körfezi the Karpas peninsula, or
panhandle as it is often called,
runs out to sea. About 45 miles
(72km) long, its very isolation
saved it from many of Cyprus's
troubles over the centuries.
Recent events illustrate most
clearly how the destiny of the
Karpas is linked to its isolation.
In 1974, Greek Cypriots in the
north fled south before the
advancing Turkish soldiers, but
not in the Karpas. Today some
550 Greek Cypriots and 250
Maronites live and go about
their business in this Turkish-
controlled area.

The drive along the peninsula
takes one past several important
ruins on the north coast,
including the ancient cities of
Karpasia and Aphendrika. On
the south side the remains of
Nektovikla can be found about
half-way along. Cyprus's
easternmost point is reached at
Zafer Burnu (Cape Apostolos
Andreas), 145 miles (233km)
from Paphos, and 70 miles
(112km) from the coast of Syria.

FAMAGUSTA
(GAZIMAGUSA)

The Turkish name for
Famagusta is Gazimagusa, but
the Greek Cypriots refer to it as
'Ammochostos' which means
'buried in sand', probably a
reference to the one-time
shifting sand dunes of the
shoreline. Two quite different

sectors make up the city which is third in size after Nicosia (Lefkosa) and Limassol. The old town is contained within walls of colossal size, an impressive legacy of the Venetian military engineers, while to the south is the modern area called Varosha. In the 1960s and up to the Turkish invasion of 1974, hotels and apartments spread rapidly along the coast, engulfing the dunes and even blotting out the sun from some stretches of beach. Today Varosha is a ghost town, still awaiting its fate.

Famagusta first came to significance with the decline of Salamis but another 600 years were to pass before it grew to any size. Thereafter it was one of the main towns of the Levant and its deepwater harbour ensured its growth as a trading centre for the countries of the eastern Mediterranean.

The town was fortified by the Lusignans and became a place of some wealth. However, by the time it was occupied by the Genoese its prosperity was declining. These new invaders were driven out in 1464 and Lusignan control restored. It was to be short-lived for in 1489 the Venetians took over the island and immediately started to rebuild the walls. Their work is what we see today.

During the Turkish siege of Famagusta in 1570-1 there was great loss of life on both sides. The following centuries saw the town deteriorate and when the British arrived in 1878 even the harbour was derelict and well silted up. Thirty years later it was dredged clean and Famagusta again became the island's main port. A recent addition to the town is the colossal Monument of Victory, near the Land Gate.

The old town has numerous old buildings of the Venetian and Lusignan eras and before, many of them unfortunately in varying stages of decay. In addition to the major sights (see **What to See** below) there are the **Biddulph's Gate** north of the cathedral, the **Djafer Pasa Baths and Fountain** by the Venetian Palace and numerous tombs of Turkish notables.

Ruins of St George of the Greeks, once Famagusta's Orthodox Cathedral

FAMAGUSTA (GAZIMAGUSA)

WHAT TO SEE

For opening times see
Directory pages 117–18.

◆
NESTORIAN CHURCH (AYIOS YEORYIOS)
northeast of the Moratto Bastion
Built in 1350 by a rich
businessman called Francis
Lakkas, the church was for the
Syrian community of Famagusta,
the Nestorians or Chaldeans
coming from Syria originally.

◆
ST GEORGE OF THE GREEKS
Mustafa Ersu Sokagi
This large church was once the
Orthodox Cathedral. Inside, its
three apses are covered with
wall paintings. The mainly
Gothic structure contrasts
strongly with the Byzantine
apses at the south end.

◆◆◆
ST NICHOLAS CATHEDRAL (LALA MUSTAFA PASA MOSQUE)
Naim Efendi Sokagi
This very fine and important
example of early 14th-century
French Gothic architecture was
built by the Lusignans. What we
see today is a splendid west
front with gables and triple
porch. Above the centre porch
is an interesting six-light window
and a rose window while the
side doors have tall blind-light
windows above them. The twin
towers have lost their tops and a
minaret has been added to the
north tower. Other additions to
the original work are two
chapels on the south side and
one on the north. The cathedral

was badly damaged in the
Ottoman siege of 1570-1, and on
its conversion to a mosque
much of the interior was
destroyed and fixtures
removed. As if this was not
enough it sustained further
damage in the earthquake of
1735. Across from the north wall
are the ruins of the
Archbishop's Palace. To the
south of the cathedral square is
a **Venetian loggia**, now with a
fountain.

◆
SINAN PASA MOSQUE (CHURCH OF ST PETER AND ST PAUL)
Sinan Pasa Sokagi
The church was built in 1358. A
system of flying buttresses
supports the nave vaulting. In
1571 it was restored, converted
to a mosque and renamed Sinan
Pasa. During British rule grain
and potatoes were stored in the
building. Further restoration
work was carried out and in
1964 the Turks used it as a Town
Hall. Eventually it was taken
over by the Ministry of
Education, Culture and Youth
and became the public library.

◆◆
VENETIAN PALACE AND NAMIK KEMAL PRISON
Sinan Pasa Sokagi
A façade of four columns
supporting three arches marks
an earlier Lusignan palace. It
was used as a prison during the
occupation by the Ottoman
Turks, one of the detainees
being the poet Namik Kemal
(1840-88). This part of the
palace is now used as a
museum in his memory.

Lala Mustafa Pasa Mosque

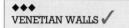

◆◆◆
VENETIAN WALLS ✓

These made Famagusta one of the strongest of the fortified cities in the Middle East. Fifteen bastions are built into the 49-foot (15m) high ramparts which are 26 feet (8m) thick in places. There is a walk along the ramparts and fantastic views over the city. Five more bastions are located along the southwest wall, these are the **Diocare**, **Moratto**, **Pulacazara** and **San Luca** bastions with the last in line, **Martinengo Bastion**, collecting the adjacent walls into a huge spearhead plan form. It is a massive construction and initially proved impregnable to the Turks in 1570. The northern walls were defended by the **Del Mozzo Bastion** and the **Diamante Bastion**.

Going seaward and passing the small **Signorina Bastion** we reach the famous **Citadel** or **'Othello's Tower'**. There is some evidence, although pretty thin, that a military governor of the island, Christophere Moro, was the Moor of Shakespeare's *Othello*. However, the tower was built in the 14th century by the Lusignans and included four subsidiary round towers at the corners. It was almost entirely surrounded by a sea-water moat. The Venetians reduced the height of the towers to fit in with the design of the great walls.

Over the entrance door by the round tower the winged lion of St Mark is carved in the stonework. Inside, a courtyard is surrounded by vaulted chambers of the Lusignan era; on one side is the impressive **Great Hall**. To the south of the tower is the **Porta del Mare** or

Sea Gate, complete with the remains of an iron portcullis. The iron-clad wooden doors date from the Ottoman Turks. From this point a long stretch of wall extends to the **Djamboulat** or **Arsenal Gate** and **Bastion** at the city's southeast corner. It was here that the Turkish General Djamboulat Bey died in the great siege. The hall of the bastion is now a museum. From here to the **Land Gate** the bastions of **Camposanto**, **Andruzzi** and **Santa Napa** punctuate the southern wall. Visitors should be aware that on the walls and in the towers there

are many unguarded openings and rickety balustrades. Great care should therefore be taken.

Accommodation

As has been made clear elsewhere most of the hotels of Famagusta are inaccessible. However, those listed below are still operating.

Altun Tabya (tel: (036) 65363), in the centre has 14 rooms and is reasonably priced. 1-star.

Palm Beach (tel: (036)

The so-called Othello's Tower, incorporated into the Venetian fortifications of Famagusta

62000/1/2) at the north end of the city has a private beach and 80 rooms. 5-star.

Panorama (tel: (036) 65880) near the walled city, has 15 rooms. 1-star.

For those who prefer independence there are 39 flats in **Laguna Beach Hotel Apartments** (tel: (036) 66502/3).

Nightlife

There is not a great deal of nightlife in this part of the island. In Famagusta the best bet is the Palm Beach hotel, which has a casino.

Restaurants

Those doing the tour of the walled city should consider calling at a cake shop a little south of the Sea Gate on Cambulat Yolu. A sweet tooth is needed for these delicious Cypriot specialities. Adjoining the shop is a tearoom. There are a few restaurants outside the old city but Famagusta is a quiet place. **Agora**, 17 Elmas Tabya sokagi (tel: (036) 65364). Genuine Turkish Cypriot food prepared in mud ovens. Closed Sunday.

Shopping

The shops of interest to the tourist are concentrated within the walled city. Here one can find attractive hand-knitted mohair sweaters at reasonable prices. Shops specialising in quality leather coats and bags are found on the busier streets. A good range of ceramics and brassware is also available. Close to the cathedral a market hides behind an interesting old colonnaded façade.

THE MESAORIA AND KARPAS

Wall mosaic in the Gymnasium, Salamis. The lyre, quiver and bow of Apollo are seen in the centre

◆◆
ENGOMI-ALASIA

5 miles (8km) north of Famagusta
Although the site looks unimpressive, the discovery of Engomi-Alasia was an exceedingly important contribution to the archaeological history of Cyprus. The earliest remains are of the 17th century BC and it may be that the city was once the capital of Cyprus. There is clear evidence that it prospered through the export of copper. Mycenaean craftsmen came to the city to produce vases and a ceramic industry gradually evolved. Unfortunately, a great fire destroyed much of the city and what remained was subsequently devastated by earthquake in the 12th century BC. Recovery proved impossible and in 100 years Engomi-Alasia was abandoned, the population

moving to Salamis.

The site was first excavated in 1896. Initially it was thought to be no more than a necropolis but subsequent excavations led to remarkable discoveries. Starting from the **North Gate** and proceeding south, the buildings discovered are the **Sanctuary of the Horned God** followed by a construction with the exciting name of **Building 18**, the **House of the Pillar** and the **House of the Bronzes**.

◆◆◆
SALAMIS

6 miles (9.5km) north of Famagusta
This is an important archaeological site and an impressive place. It is an

essential visit any time but in high summer the burning heat and dazzling light combine to make it a memorable experience.

Salamis was a city-kingdom, its exact date of origin unknown. However, various artefacts discovered on the site date from the 11th century BC. The rise of Salamis to prominence only took place when the nearby settlement of Engomi-Alasia (see opposite) was abandoned following severe damage by earthquake. It rapidly became the most influential of the kingdoms of Cyprus, remaining so for over a thousand years. The early rulers of Salamis found it necessary to stand out against the encroachments of many of the powerful forces of the eastern Mediterranean.

When the Persians suffered an irretrievable reverse by Alexander the Great at Tyre in 322BC, a desperate struggle for possession of Cyprus followed, from which the Ptolemies, the Hellenistic dynasty of Egypt, emerged victorious. They ruled until the Romans arrived in 58BC, establishing a domination that lasted until AD395.

Salamis, while continuing as an important commercial centre under the Romans, gradually lost its position as the main city of the island to Paphos. Nevertheless, the eventful history of Salamis continued. Severe earthquakes in AD76 and 77 caused much damage. In the 4th century earthquakes and tidal waves finally left Salamis in ruins. A new city was commissioned by the Byzantine

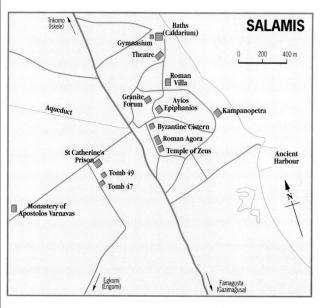

SALAMIS

Trikomo (Iskele)

Baths (Caldarium)

Gymnasium

Theatre

Roman Villa

Granite Forum

Ayios Epiphanios

Kampanopetra

Aqueduct

Byzantine Cistern

Roman Agora

St Catherine's Prison

Temple of Zeus

Ancient Harbour

Tomb 49

Tomb 47

Monastery of Apostolos Varnavas

Egkomi (Engomi)

Famagusta (Gazimağusa)

0   200   400 m

N

THE MESAORIA AND KARPAS

Emperor Constantine and called Constantia. In the 7th century it was sacked by Arabs and finally abandoned, the inhabitants fleeing to Famagusta.

The city lay beneath the sands for centuries and it was not until 1880 that the first excavations took place; they have continued on and off ever since.

The ruins are in two distinct sections separated by the main road. To the west is a necropolis, to the east the ancient city itself. Three groups of ruins can be identified. Close to the main road is the **Roman Agora** and the **Temple of Zeus**. Over on the east is the **Kampanopetra** and **Ancient Harbour**. To the north are the **gymnasium**, **baths** and **theatre**. Access from the main highway is signposted and along a good road. Visitors should decide whether or not to travel throughout on foot or to make use of their car. Some people may wish to spend all day at the site. It should be appreciated that the distance from the gymnasium to the Temple of Zeus is no less than 1,000 yards (900m).

Beaches

Famagusta's splendid main beach is now inaccessible. There is, however, a stretch of sand next to the Palm Beach Hotel, a little to the north. From Famagusta to Salamis there lies **Clapsides** beach and one or two others. Moving north, a good sandy beach runs along the shore by the ruins of **Salamis**. Close to the ancient site, the Salamis Bay Hotel has a fine stretch of sand.

Various narrow beaches line the bay before it sweeps into the unspoilt Karpas peninsula, which has small beaches on either side. Towards Zafer Burnu (Cape Apostolos Andreas), the furthest extremity, there is a stretch of sand dunes. Visitors should check with the Tourist Office whether access is still restricted.

Accommodation

Visitors to this part of the island tend to prefer the coast around Salamis to Famagusta itself. Two hotels near the ruins are:
Park (tel: (036) 65511), 7 miles (11km) from Famagusta. Has a private beach. 4-star.
Salamis Bay (tel: (036) 76201/6), 11 miles (18km) from Famagusta. A large hotel with a private beach. 360 rooms. 4-star.
For the independent-minded there are the **Dagli Hotel Apartments** near Salamis (tel: (036) 67864), with 9 flats. Even further up the coast, 16 miles (26km) northwest of Famagusta, at the village of Bogaz is:
Hotel View (tel: (0371) 2651) with 30 rooms and private beach. 4-star.

Nightlife

The Salamis Bay Hotel is probably the best hope for evening entertainment. It is a huge complex and has bars and a discothèque.

Restaurants

The EYVA restaurant near the Salamis ruins serves a variety of local dishes. At Bogaz, 5 miles (8km) north of Salamis is **Carli's** (tel: (037) 12515). Fish restaurant; good views.

PEACE AND QUIET

Wildlife and Countryside on Cyprus
by Paul Sterry

Cyprus has much to offer the visiting naturalist: a good range of the more typical Mediterranean plants and animals can easily be found and, because of its geographical position and wide range of habitats, several unique species occur. The island serves as a staging post for migration to and from Europe and Africa, and hundreds of thousands of birds pass through the island in spring and autumn. This amazing spectacle is marred only by the widespread hunting of songbirds.

A chequered history of invasion and occupation has left its mark in ways which affect not only the island's inhabitants, but also its visitors. The division of the island and the military presence inevitably mean that certain areas are particularly sensitive. It would be unwise, therefore, to use binoculars or a camera close to the border, around strategic sites within the British Sovereign Base Areas and near the listening stations like the one at Mount Olympus. Signs prohibiting these pursuits are generally prominent.

The Coast and Sea
The limestone coastline is

Spectacular, waveworn cliffs and crystal-clear sea at Cape Greco

PEACE AND QUIET

You are likely to see Cyprus warblers flitting among the branches in such places as old olive groves

generally rocky and, in places, has been eroded by wave action to form sea caves and strange pinnacles. Elsewhere, where conditions are more suitable, sandy beaches composed of pure white sand have formed and these are soon colonised by maritime plants. The azure waters of the Mediterranean have a small tidal range, which means that little evidence of marine life is exposed at low tide. However, beneath the surface of the water, marine life thrives, and colourful fishes and anemones can be seen with a simple snorkel and mask.

Sea birds are comparatively scarce in the Mediterranean generally, but around Cyprus, Cory's shearwaters and the eastern Mediterranean race of Manx shearwater may occasionally be seen. Both are superb flyers, using their stiff wings to glide effortlessly over the sea in search of surface marine life. This reliance on the wind means that onshore winds often bring these and other seabirds close to the coast, and cliffs around **Ayia Napa** in the southwest of the island and around Paphos, and headlands such as **Cape Kiti** south of Larnaca, are particularly good. Jackdaws and rock doves frequent these cliffs and three stretches of coast have breeding colonies of Eleonora's falcons, whose aerobatic skills are a joy to watch.

Lesser black-backed, slender-billed and Audouin's gulls may also be seen on occasions and are sometimes lured to harbours such as Limassol, together with black-headed and herring gulls. Gulls and shearwaters are seen on ferry crossings to Haifa in Israel or Latakia in Syria, and there is always a chance of seeing dolphins bow-riding alongside the boat.

Many of the beaches between Larnaca and Cape Greco are popular with tourists, and suffer from considerable disturbance. However, drive away from the main centres and comparatively deserted beaches such as those at **Pissouri Bay** near Cape Aspro or **Khrysokhou Bay** can be found. Sand dunes are soon colonised by plants, and marram grass, spurges and stocks add a splash of colour in spring. On a few isolated beaches, Kentish plovers may try to nest, while breeding loggerhead turtles are now reduced to one beach near Paphos where they are strictly protected (see page 46). Formerly widespread, these immense marine reptiles lay their eggs in the sand and human disturbance now excludes them from most areas.

Agricultural Land

Many parts of coastal Cyprus support a thriving agriculture. Red, fertile soils north of Larnaca Bay produce melons and potatoes, the latter serving as food for the larvae of death's head hawk moths, while land to the west of Limassol is famous for its oranges. Elsewhere, olive groves, fig trees and pomegranates produce a rich harvest, while many hill slopes are covered in vineyards. Fortunately, since the farming is not especially intensive, wildlife can often live in harmony with the agricultural practices. However, farmland suffers more than most areas from the indiscriminate slaughter of songbirds for which Cyprus has such a bad reputation. Overgrown orchards and olive groves are the haunt of little owls, which nest in cracks and holes in the gnarled trees. Endemic Cyprus warblers, considered by some to be a race of the widespread Sardinian warbler, search the foliage for insects and are found in similar sites to olivaceous warblers, which are summer visitors to the island. Early April

also sees the arrival of masked shrikes to Cyprus, these beautifully marked birds nesting among the dense foliage. Overhead wires serve as ideal lookouts for resident kestrels, as well as migrant lesser kestrels and red-footed falcons. Bee-eaters and rollers also survey the terrain for insect quarry, while black-headed buntings use the wires as song perches from which to advertise their territories.

Abandoned orchards soon develop a rich undergrowth of spring flowers – poppies and corn marigolds – which are visited by colourful butterflies, and an abundance of grasses. Corn buntings find these conditions ideal, and the meadows sometimes harbour quails whose 'wet-my-lips' call is often the only clue as to their presence. In the autumn and winter, the seeds are a rich source of food for goldfinches, larks and house sparrows, and flocks of the latter should be carefully scrutinised for Spanish sparrows.

Bare, arable fields are the haunt of crested larks, hooded crows and magpies. In spring, hoopoes and several different races of yellow wagtail may be found, while in winter there is a large influx of migrant birds from northern Europe.

Open Country

Before man colonised Cyprus, most of the land would have been covered in evergreen forests, but only pockets of woodland remain today. On soil that could not support agriculture, tree regeneration

PEACE AND QUIET

was prevented by grazing animals, and an open and colourful community of specialised plants, known as *phrygana,* developed along with a range of interesting animals. This habitat is mainly restricted to the coastal lowlands, and good areas are found in the west of the island and also between Limassol and Cape Kiti. For much of the year, the vegetation may look parched and dead, with only evergreen leaves giving a hint of life. From January to May, however, the plants produce an abundance of flowers with thyme, rosemary, cistus and sage catching the eye. One of the most exciting features of the *phrygana* on Cyprus is its range of orchids. Helleborines, giant orchids and Crimean orchids are all striking and comparatively large, but members of the bee orchid family, although small, are beautifully marked. In particular, the yellow bee orchid is extremely attractive, and the Cyprus bee orchid, *Ophrys kotschyi,* is endemic. Although not abundant, the birdlife of the *phrygana* is of special interest to the naturalist. In addition to common species, like linnet and hooded crow, this habitat also supports the Cyprus race of pied wheatear throughout most of the island and Cretzschmar's bunting at high altitudes. Areas of low-growing vegetation sometimes harbour spectacled warblers while bushes and shrubs are favoured by the endemic Cyprus warbler, a boldly marked black and white bird.

Freshwater Habitats

In common with most other areas of the Mediterranean, freshwater is at a premium, with rainfall being almost unknown between May and September. During the summer months, many of the rivers dry up and coastal lagoons, such as at Akrotiri and Larnaca, become ever more saline. Finding enough water is a problem not only for much of Cyprus's wildlife, but also for its people, and to combat the threat of drought, reservoirs and dams have been built. These maintain a constant supply for the population, and also serve to attract a variety of wildlife which might otherwise be difficult to find.

Where river mouths meet the sea around the coast, the banks are often lined with marshes, and large reedbeds sometimes develop. Where development has not affected them, they come alive in spring with a chorus of male frogs, which serves to attract not only mates but also predators such as herons, egrets and snakes. Competing in voice with the frogs are reed warblers, fan-tailed warblers and Cetti's warblers, the song of the latter being extremely loud and explosive.

As the summer drought approaches and the rivers dry up, some animals move to different areas or seek a retreat. Many species of snail, however, go into a form of summer 'hibernation' known as aestivation, and large clumps of them adorn the stems of plants. Migrant birds sometimes follow the courses of rivers inland, and so, in spring, it is worth checking the riverside vegetation for warblers. Lucky observers may come across black francolins, which are particularly fond of dry river courses and the margins of drying lakes. This species, more than most on Cyprus, has suffered a severe decline in numbers, largely due to hunting pressure, and is rather difficult to find.

In the Troodos Mountains, the **Prodhromos Reservoir** is surrounded by forest, while reservoirs lower down, such as **Yermasoyia Dam**, northeast of Limassol, and **Athalassa Dam**, near Nicosia, although perhaps less attractive, lure a great range of birds. In the summer months, red-rumped swallows and swifts may be found hawking insects over the surface, while, around the margins, birds such as goldfinch and serin come to drink and bathe. During migration, waders and terns pass through, and in winter the waters attract migrant wildfowl, coots and little grebes.

The Cyprus bee orchid is an exciting find. This beautiful species of orchid grows nowhere else

The Forests

Throughout the Mediterranean, forests provide welcome shade from the baking sun during the summer months, and those on Cyprus are no exception. The main area of woodland is the **Paphos Forest** in the west of the island, but there are patches elsewhere throughout Cyprus, all with interesting birds, insects and plants. Until earlier this century, the forests had suffered a sad decline: areas were cleared without any control and

regeneration of seedlings was almost entirely prevented by grazing goats. Fortunately, the forest station at **Stavros tis Psokas** was established to control regeneration and replanting in the Paphos Forest. At higher elevations in the Paphos Forest, black or Troodos pine is common, but on the lower slopes, and elsewhere in the island, Aleppo pine predominates. Dense stands of woodland have a forest floor carpeted with pine needles, which the occasional orchid pushes through in spring. In glades and clearings, however, a rich community of plants develops with cistuses, heathers

PEACE AND QUIET

and lavenders perfuming the air.

Butterflies like the Cleopatra and scarce swallowtail visit the flowers and, where the strawberry tree is present as a larval foodplant, the two-tailed pasha glides through the air. In sunny, lowland clearings, clumps of caper may be found, easily recognisable by its large, white flowers with protruding violet stamens. This is the caper used in the kitchen: unopened flowers and unripe seeds are used in salads and sauces, or to flavour pickles.

Woodlands can be rich in birdlife, although a considerable amount of effort may be needed to see some of the more skulking species. Common woodland birds include serin, chaffinch, greenfinch, wren, great tit and coal tit, which tend to breed in woods at higher elevations, but disperse to lowland areas in the winter. Patient observation may also reveal short-toed treecreepers or crossbills, the latter being almost entirely dependent on the seeds of pines.

Summer visitors to woodlands include two birds, the Scop's owl and golden oriole, perhaps best known for their songs. That of the owl is a monotonous whistle, which can go on all night long, while the golden oriole's song is rich and fluty, and one of the finest of all European birds. Where thickets of scrub-like vegetation develop in clearings and glades, you may find the endemic Cyprus warbler or the bulky olivaceous warbler.

Spring Flowers
In common with the rest of the Mediterranean, Cyprus enjoys long, hot summers with almost

The caterpillars of the two-tailed pasha butterfly feed on strawberry trees, so the adults are likely to be seen where this tree grows

no prospect of rain from May until September. While this may favour the tourist trade, the heat and drought present severe problems for flowering plants. Those that are able to survive, do so thanks to centuries of adaptation and most take advantage of the mild and comparatively wet winter and early spring to grow, flower and set seed. The landscape in August is parched and dry, but return again any time from January to April and lush, green vegetation and colourful flowers greet the eye.

Tall, white flower spikes of asphodel are one of the most conspicuous features of areas of cultivated land while beneath them, poppies, grape hyacinths, tassel hyacinths and flowers of paper-white narcissus nod in the breeze. Starry clover, Jersey cudweed and larkspur often thrive in the most unpromising areas, sometimes right beside a road or track.

Where fields are left undisturbed for any length of time, for instance in areas of abandoned orchards, colourful meadows soon develop. In early spring, these may be a sea of corn marigold, crown daisy, corn chamomile with gladioli, irises, beard grass, hare's tail grass and large quaking grass completing the display.

While many plants tolerate disturbance, some indeed thriving on it, others take longer to develop and only grow on undisturbed ground. Open, stony places are ideal for crocuses and crown anemones, while cyclamens and the curiously shaped friar's cowl prefer a degree of shade. Most characteristic of the spring flowers of undisturbed soils, however, are the orchids of which more than 20 species are found on Cyprus. The giant orchid, *Barlia robertiana* and numerous members of the bee orchid family are widespread, while many of the helleborines are restricted to the mountains.

The Akrotiri Peninsula

Lying to the south of Limassol, the Akrotiri Peninsula is dominated by a large salt lake but also comprises some excellent areas of scrub, beaches and rocky shore. The whole area lies within the British Sovereign Base Area which has probably benefited the wildlife through reduced hunting and disturbance. However, the military presence also means that the southern half of the peninsula is not easily accessible to the public and the use of binoculars or cameras is inadvisable or prohibited in places.

The salt lake, famous for its wintering flamingos and renowned locally for its vicious mosquitoes, is best viewed either from tracks to the east or on foot from the road to the west. Around the margins of the lake, water-loving birds such as little egrets, squacco herons and glossy ibises feed in the open, while more secretive little bitterns and purple herons occasionally creep into view or are seen in flight. The surrounding tamarisk scrub, above which fan-tailed warblers sing, harbours newly arrived migrant songbirds at the right

PEACE AND QUIET

times of year and persistent observers may find Dead Sea sparrows. A breeding population of these summer visitors to Cyprus was first discovered in 1980 – an exciting addition to the island's list of birds.

Flamingos are most regularly seen between October and February when several thousand birds may be present along with large numbers of wildfowl. **Akrotiri Salt Lake** is the best site on Cyprus for flamingos and one of the most important wintering areas in the eastern Mediterranean, but despite the protection that it supposedly enjoys together with **Larnaca Salt Lake**, birds are still killed by hunters.

During spring and autumn, the lake hosts the greatest variety of species with migrant waders such as black-winged stilt, dunlin, ruff and little stint as well as more unusual species like marsh sandpiper and broad-billed sandpiper. Flocks of white-winged black terns and red-rumped swallows catch insects on the wing, signs of alarm in their behaviour sometimes indicating a passing griffon vulture, Eleonora's falcon or a migrant pallid harrier.

The sea around the Akrotiri Peninsula is full of marine life and the southern end of Lady's Mile Beach is worth exploring. Divers regularly feed the fish and so, with the aid of snorkel and mask, visitors can see amazingly colourful fish such as mullet and wrasse, as well as octopuses, plumose anemones, starfishes, sea urchins and sea slugs.

Larnaca and Adjacent Areas
The coastal town of Larnaca is ideally placed for exploring a range of different habitats. Beaches, dunes and rocky headlands fringe the coast while near by are salt lakes and marshes which are excellent for the birdwatcher.

To the south of Larnaca lies a series of salt lakes which attract an interesting range of migrant and wintering birds. The northern lake, which is the largest, is well below sea-level and is still mined for salt to this day. A road crosses its southern edge and to the south of this and Larnaca Airport is a series of smaller lakes and pools which are generally the best sites for birdwatching. Flamingos are regularly present in the winter months from October until March, although their exact numbers and dates of arrival and departure are somewhat unpredictable.

Spring migration, from March to May, is particularly rewarding as far as waders are concerned, although autumn is not without its highlights. Little stints, ruff and little-ringed plovers mingle with black-winged stilts and wood sandpipers and careful observation may reveal a broad-billed sandpiper or greater sandplover. Egrets and herons feed around the margins and at dusk patience may produce a brief glimpse of a little crake.

To the west of the northern lake lies the mosque known as **Hala Sultan Tekke** (see page 20) from which good views can be had of the water. Although the surrounding lakeside vegetation is good for birds such as Cetti's warbler, the grounds in which the mosque lies should not be neglected. Cicadas serenade from the trees and bushes which include colourful species such as mimosa (actually a species of *Acacia*). This peaceful and unspoilt haven is sometimes 'alive' with migrant birds and the flowers attract day-flying hummingbird hawk moths.

To the north of the town lies **Larnaca Bay** where, in places, sand dunes have been colonised by marram grass. The shifting sand having been stabilised, other flowers such as spurges, stock, centaury and mallow-leaved bindweed can soon colonise, producing a colourful array of flowers in early spring. By the summer, most of the vegetation has turned brown in the heat but in late summer, flowers of the sea daffodil and sea squill appear, showing that life still survives. During periods of strong onshore winds, seabirds may be seen offshore but **Cape Kiti** to the south of Larnaca is a more reliable spot for the dedicated seawatcher.

The Troodos Mountains
The centre of western Cyprus is dominated by the Troodos Mountains, a series of peaks with panoramic views rising to 6,401 feet (1,951m) above sea-level at Mount Olympus. The pleasant summer temperatures offer a welcome change from the searing heat on the coast, while in winter regular snowfalls have turned the area into a ski resort. The climate also suits a considerable variety of wildlife and many species of plants, birds and mammals have the Troodos as their main centre of distribution on Cyprus.

Once common, Cyprus moufflon are now found only in Paphos Forest

PEACE AND QUIET

Vineyards and olive groves cover some of the lower slopes but, particularly at higher elevations, there is a considerable amount of natural woodland. The black pine, or Troodos pine, is widespread at higher altitudes as are oriental plane and maple. A few cedars still survive and can be seen in Cedar Valley and around nearby Kykko Monastery. They often support singing serins and chaffinches during the summer. Although the soil is generally broken and stony, shady woodland clearings are often good for plants such as the aromatic ploughman's spikenard (*Dittrichia viscosa*) as well as a variety of orchids. Violet limodore, small white orchid, red helleborine and Anatolian orchid are all comparatively widespread in the Mediterranean but the scarce marsh helleborine (*Epipactis veratrifolia*) is more local, while the Cyprus helleborine (*Epipactis troodii*) is a species found only in this part of the island.

Clearings often support a wide variety of low-growing, aromatic plants as well as showy species like red valerian, sage and French lavender which attract butterflies and day-flying moths. The onset of autumn heralds the emergence of large numbers of fungi and edible species are eagerly harvested by local people, who regard them as a delicacy.

Crag martins feed around rocky outcrops, catching insects on the wing, while parties of common, pallid or alpine swifts race through the skies at greater heights. A variety of birds of prey pass through the area on migration and patient observation may also produce sightings of resident griffon vultures, as well as rare glimpses of peregrine, Bonelli's eagle or imperial eagle. Stony ground in the Troodos is ideal for Cretzschmar's bunting, while forested thickets may be occupied by singing nightingales, their song being rivalled only by the woodlark.

The Cyprus Moufflon

The Cyprus moufflon (*Ovis aries ovion*) is one of the ancestors of modern-day sheep and is similar in appearance to traditional rare breeds such as the Soay sheep. Although introduced to other parts of the Mediterranean from populations on Sardinia and Corsica, moufflon were at one time only known on Cyprus and these two other islands. The history of the Cyprus moufflon is a sadly familiar one: once hunted almost to the point of extinction, it still survives in small numbers near the forest station at Stavros tis Psokas in the Paphos Forest. Open, Aleppo pine woodland is the preferred habitat where the animals live in small herds and would, under normal conditions, move up the slopes in the summer months. Individuals are smaller than the other relict populations of races on Corsica and Sardinia but the males still possess wonderfully curved horns.

Cyprus has restaurants for all tastes. This is the dining room of the Nereus Sunotel in Paphos

FOOD AND DRINK

Cypriots have an enthusiasm for running their own businesses. As a result there are numerous individual restaurants and cafés all over Cyprus.

In the choice of restaurants there is something for everyone. The cautious tourist who likes his food much as at home will have no difficulty finding a good restaurant to provide something acceptably close. Also, there is no difficulty in the main resorts getting hamburger or pizza with chips. However, not all Cypriots are into this sort of food, and there are scores of restaurants that provide excellent local dishes although some are a little off the beaten track.

Most eating in summer is al fresco; restaurants can vary from a few tables and chairs under the vines to more permanent and elaborate places. Indoor establishments of the more formal variety are relatively few, except in Nicosia and perhaps Limassol. All bills come with a 10 per cent service charge, a 3 per cent Cyprus Tourism Organisation tax, and 5 per cent VAT. With the fall in the pound sterling and these new taxes, Cyprus is becoming expensive.

What is on the Menu?

Greek and Turkish Cypriot food is similar in many ways but has different names. Pork and ham are hard to come by in the north. Below are some favourite Greek dishes and a few Turkish ones. In the tourist areas most menus are presented with an English translation.

In Cyprus **mezedhes** *(meze),* meaning 'mixture', is the thing, as it is of course in Greece. It is remarkable how quickly the uninitiated develop a taste for this collection of hot and cold appetisers, served in small dishes. It can of course be taken as a meal in its own right. The early part of the meal will include a variety of dips such as fish roe paste **(taramosalata)**; yoghurt and cucumber **(tzatsiki)**; sesame seed paste **(tashinosalata)**; a purée of chick-peas, olive oil and hot spices **(houmous)**; and several

FOOD AND DRINK

others. Olives will be much in evidence and probably spicy squid and smoked sausages and skewered pieces of lamb, not to mention the famous **halloumi** cheese. These interesting dishes arrive one after the other over a fairly lengthy period, so take care not to overdo it early on. There is difficulty in breaking with custom and refusing dishes, but sleep does not come easy to those who imprudently take too much of a late *mezedhes*.

Simple **kebab** is as popular with the Cypriots as most things. The pieces of meat are skewered and roasted over a slow charcoal fire and eaten in an envelope of pitta bread. Another favourite is **kleftico**. This is lamb, usually cooked very slowly in a sealed earthenware pot. In the villages *kleftico* ovens are used – beehive constructions made

A selection of Cypriot wines

with baked mud. Most people will have heard of **moussaka** and Cyprus is a good place to try this dish of mince, aubergines and béchamel sauce.

Of the soups **avgolemono** is a more adventurous choice than the mixed vegetable. The former is chicken broth with lemon juice, thickened with eggs and served with rice. Alternatively try **stifado**, a stew of beef, tomato and onion. Fresh pasta is popular, a speciality being **kypriakes ravioles**, ravioli stuffed with *halloumi* cheese, mint and eggs. The welcome Cypriots accord to visitors is not extended to feathered migrants. Many are shot but the poor blackcap known as **ambelopoulia** is caught on lime-sticks and its insignificant carcass pickled and served up as a great delicacy. At all meals the locals pile side plates high with good fresh salad.

For those with a sweet tooth Cypriot desserts are irresistible, for most are exceedingly sweet. **Baklava** is a pastry with nuts, syrup and cinnamon. **Kadeifi** has a similar filling in a casing which looks rather like a loofah. A big favourite is **soujoukko**, where strings of nuts are dipped into grape juice and allowed to set. It is much in evidence at village fairs where it is sold in varying lengths.

Fish is something of a disappointment; the choice of fresh fish is often limited to swordfish and red mullet, red snapper and a small fish called *psirika,* although in the Troodos hills trout from the fish farms is readily available. Squid, lobster and shrimp are available but are likely to be frozen rather than fresh. All the seafood, whether grilled, stuffed, or sautéed is relatively expensive. No Cypriot would contemplate finishing a meal without Turkish coffee (called Greek coffee in some quarters since the troubles of 1974). It comes in a tiny cup with a glass of water and is taken sweet, medium or unsweetened; never with milk.

Most of the above dishes have their Turkish counterparts. **Sis kebap** is lamb roasted on a skewer and served up with tomatoes and rice. **Doner kebap** is lamb or beef roasted on a huge turning skewer and then thinly cut.

Drinks

All wines seem to taste good on location, but all too often the bottles carried home fail to come up to expectations. Some Cypriot wines will definitely fall into this category; others are good and improving.

Commandaria St John is a name long associated with Cyprus. First produced for the Knights of St John at Kolossi, it is a sweet fortified dessert wine. The white wines of the island are mainly dry; among them are **Keo Hock**, **White Lady**, **Arsinoe** and **Aphrodite**. In the reds there is plenty of choice. **Othello** is a great favourite and so is **Afames**. None of these wines are available in the north. There are a few locally produced varieties including **Kantara White** and **Red**, products of the recently created wine industry. Other wines are

imported from Turkey and Europe.

Light beer is exceedingly refreshing on hot days. The locally made **Keo** is available everywhere in the south. **Carlsberg** is very similar, although experts claim they can tell the difference by the nature and intensity of the hangover. In the north all the beer is from Turkey or further afield.

Brandy is made locally in large quantities and consumed in equally large quantities after dinner, and at other times, as a brandy sour, where it is mixed with lemon juice, bitters and soda water. **Ouzo** is a powerful aniseed-flavoured drink and needs approaching with caution. **Filfar**, an orange liqueur, is an alternative to brandy as an after-dinner drink.

SHOPPING

Of the resorts, Limassol has the most varied and best shopping, competing with Nicosia.

The Cypriots are enthusiastic about craftwork and many shops display the best examples. Baskets of varying sizes in rush or cane are reasonably priced. Ceramics can be a good buy: especially eye-catching are the terracotta statuettes, some of the designs being clearly inspired by the ancient works of art found in Cyprus. Pots and hand-thrown jars from Kornos and Phini are also worthy.

Carpets and curtains have some distinctive but simple patterns, some with a definite oriental look. Unfortunately, they do not lend themselves to easy packing in a suitcase.

SHOPPING

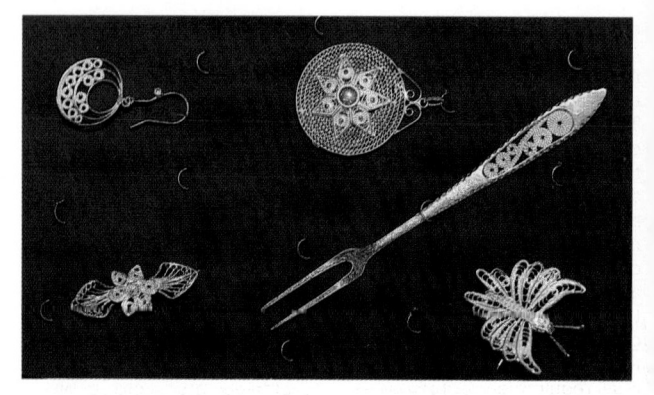

The Greeks call the island Kypros, which may derive from the Greek word for copper. A copper industry has certainly existed in Cyprus for thousands of years and this tradition in copperware continues today, much of it still hand crafted. Interesting examples of brass candlesticks and trays stand alongside the copper items. The renowned Cyprus lace (known as *lefkaritika*) or embroidery is of course to be seen in many shops. Most of it is from famous Lefkara, but some comes from Phiti in western Cyprus. Shoes and sandals seem to be something of a Cypriot speciality for there is a tremendous selection of locally designed items. Shops with hundreds of leather bags hanging from on high are located in all the towns. Designs come in all shapes and sizes and suit a multitude of applications. Some of the jewellery shops, especially in Nicosia, have some interesting work in silver and gold.

The Cyprus Handicraft Service is a government-run body that

Fine metal objects in copper or, as here, in silver, make good-value purchases in Cyprus

can offer advice to tourists about Cypriot handicrafts. Their showrooms offer a range of locally produced crafts for sale. The main centre is in Nicosia at 186 Athalassa Avenue, but other outlets are in Larnaca, Limassol and Paphos.

Cyprus is not short on opticians and they are all capable of carrying out eye tests with the latest equipment. The range of frames and lenses offered compares well in design and quality with most other places and at much lower cost.

In the past, Cyprus was renowned for tailors that could produce a suit within 24 hours, a claim not made so often now. Most of these family tailoring shops are found in the old parts of Nicosia and Limassol.

Supermarkets exist in all the towns and where there is a concentration of holiday developments. In the south they are as good as supermarkets anywhere, if not quite so enormous as some. Nevertheless, the best place for fresh fruit and vegetables is usually the open air markets. The ubiquitous stall or kiosk deserves a mention. Wherever there are shops or people the stall is not far away. Apart from magazines and newspapers most have an amazing selection of bric-à-brac. Others specialise in food, selling a variety of toasted sandwiches, etc. Many goods and services are subject to 5 per cent VAT. There is no legal requirement for prices desplayed to include this – it will be added on at the till. For shop hours see **Opening Times** (pages 116-17).

ACCOMMODATION

There are a tremendous number of rooms in southern Cyprus; hotels and apartments are everywhere. Despite this accommodation can be scarce at the height of the season when most rooms in hotels are taken by package tours. Prices can be relatively high, though last minute bookings are possible. For the independent traveller the disadvantages are that the package hotels are often out of town, do not cater for overnight stays, and are perhaps a little expensive. The true budget traveller will therefore find that cheap clean hotels are not in plentiful supply; perhaps three or four in each of the coastal towns. Nicosia is different; there are many cheap and not so cheap old hotels, although some of them are to be avoided, and a few large modern hotels. Backpackers can now be seen

in Cyprus, mainly in the west and generally using the growing number of campsites.

In the south, all the officially registered hotels are listed in the Cyprus Tourism Organisation's *Guide to Hotels*, freely available from the Cyprus Tourist Offices on the island and abroad. This booklet is absolutely essential for the independent traveller. The hotels are classified in a 1- to 5-star rating, hotels without a star, guest houses and hotel apartments, youth hostels and even campsites. Full details including prices are given. There is, unfortunately, no way of knowing from the booklet which are good or bad and some are dubious to say the least.

In northern Cyprus accommodation is limited and relatively expensive. There are several excellent hotels and apartments in and near Kyrenia and likewise Famagusta. A pamphlet by the North Cyprus Tourist Office, which lists all the hotels and apartments and their facilities, is available from North Cyprus Tourist Office (for addresses, see page 121). Reception areas often give a

---

Arriving without accommodation
Make sure you are in possession of the Tourist Office booklet *'Guide to Hotels'*. On disembarkation ask a taxi driver to take you to a nearby hotel (enquire as to the cost of the fare and the likely cost of the room before setting off).

clue to what a hotel is like, although deterioration can set in with every floor climbed. Before anything irrevocable is done, the room should be looked at. Visitors can stay at the monasteries for a night or two, but not all take women.
For the young and the hardy, there are a few campsites and youth hostels. For details, see **Directory** pages 110 and 120.

CULTURE, ENTERTAINMENT AND NIGHTLIFE

Nicosia's Municipal Theatre stages plays in Greek and English and also concerts. The Roman Theatre at Kourion (page 29) is the venue for public performances of music and drama during the summer months, details of which will be supplied by the Tourist Offices. From time to time the British Council in Nicosia puts on various entertainments by visiting theatre companies and celebrities.
In the resorts there are bars, tavernas and discothèques, the latter often being part of hotel complexes. A big town like Limassol has much more going on than, say, Larnaca. In Ayia Napa, exclusively a 'holiday town', life goes on until the early hours and some people go straight from the night-clubs to the beach. In the north, Kyrenia has a preponderance of casinos. Many simply house a collection of one-armed bandits and pin tables, but two hotels have roulette and blackjack, etc. Many tavernas in the south have their own traditional dance group. At some time in the evening visitors will be encouraged to take the

floor *en masse* and join in, probably to the tune of *Zorba the Greek*. The steps are not difficult and with a little liquid fortification a successful time may be had. Plate-throwing sessions fell into disfavour during the hard times of 1974, but this mayhem can occasionally break out.
Quite a few of the hotels put on a range of entertainment. There are folk evenings, cabarets and of course barbecues. The sound of the *bouzouki,* a kind of mandolin originating in Greece, is never far away in the late evening. Most of the bigger hotels (3-star and above) have resident bands for anyone wishing to foxtrot and rumba through the evening. Nicosia is not a resort town, so organised entertainment specially for visitors is not common. There are of course discothèques and a night-club or two, plus some famous bars, the latter invariably failing to live up to their reputation. What Nicosia does have is cinemas, some of them open air in summer. Limassol is similar in this respect. The films are usually in English with Greek subtitles.

WEATHER AND WHEN TO GO

Cyprus is the most easterly of the Mediterranean islands and as a consequence is the driest and hottest. In summer it is very hot. The temperature starts to build up in May and by July and August it is up to 30°C (90°F) on the coast and quite a bit higher inland (over 38°C/100°F in Nicosia). There is no chance of rain from June to September and rain in May and October is exceedingly unlikely. In the summer months at sea-level only the lightest of clothing is needed. Cypriots do wear suits occasionally in the hot months but it has to be for a very special formal event. In the mountains it is a different story, for early and late summer nights – although certainly not the days – can be quite cold. In winter, jackets and sweaters are needed at high or low altitude. Swimmers will be pleased to know that the sea is warm from early June to the end of October. Winter bathing is a breathtaking experience and only for the hardy.

Perhaps the most important consideration for visitors is the cut-off point between reliable weather and the possibility of bad. If the idea of a Mediterranean holiday is warm sun, drinks on the terrace and shorts, then November through to the beginning of April is out. Quite apart from everywhere being closed, it gets dark far too early and December, January and February are certain to get some rain. Winter evenings are cold and (away from the new hotels) heating systems can be primitive or kept on at half power by proprietors wearing two or even three sweaters. Hill walkers should also be wary of winter, for between good days the mountains are often wet and shrouded in mist. Proper equipment is necessary at this time of year.

April is the month to witness the famous Cyprus spring when the landscape is transformed into a blaze of colour. There is a chance of rain and the sea has not warmed up, but it can be splendidly warm; a good time for getting about, as is the month of May and late September. From June onward the land becomes brown and parched, although the trees retain a dusty greenery.

To the dismay of sailors and windsurfers, Cyprus is not a windy place. A good blow can be found off the capes but nowhere else. Sunbathers will rarely be driven off the beach as they might be, for example, in Crete.

NICOSIA (LEFKOŞA)

December - February

April - October

HOW TO BE A LOCAL

From the outset, it should be appreciated that a Cypriot's view of things can be, in some respects, less complicated or sophisticated than that of the average visitor. Business matters, for instance, are conducted face to face; letters, no matter how polite, demanding or grovelling, do not have anything like the same effect and are often completely ignored. If somebody owes you money you go and ask

HOW TO BE A LOCAL

for it; after a coffee – two if necessary – you get paid. That is the system.

This philosophy extends to personal relations. Here and now are what matter, and the future . . . well, it might be postponed or cancelled. For example, after an initial meeting with a local, two weeks later you might not remember his name, but almost certainly he would remember yours. In a further two years, the roles are likely to be reversed.

To get the best out of the Cypriots you have to be present.

It does not take long to realise that rules and regulations do not impress the locals. This can lead to a somewhat insouciant attitude to road traffic matters. For instance, Cypriot drivers consider that if you are in your car and reach your destination, you stop and get out regardless of external factors. This certainly takes the headache out of parking.

On the beach or picnicking in the woods, locals rarely seek out a quiet hideaway, but just sit down right next to somebody who is already there. That the site is otherwise empty as far as the eye can see is no matter. Privacy has never been high on the list of priorities of the people of eastern countries.

The Cypriots appreciate visitors' attempts to speak their language. However, if they speak good English it is best not to persist after the first fulsome praise. For a start they may get bored, but worst still and however ridiculous, it could be construed that their English is not good enough.

There is a great tradition of hospitality in the Middle East, and food and drink should not be refused. Conversely it should always be offered to locals when they are your guests. One way *not* to be a local is to consume vast quantities of drink and cavort through the town. Although Cypriots drink lots of brandy in the villages they can make a glass of beer last all night and rarely show signs of real inebriation. Along with most resorts in the Mediterranean, the beaches in Cyprus, even in the north, have gone topless. However, full nudity is not permitted.

In churches, monasteries and mosques appropriate dress should be worn. This means that shorts and bare shoulders are out.

Visitors can give offence by inadvertently implying, however indirectly, that some aspect of Cyprus is not up to standard. Leave such criticism to the real locals.

Of course one very good way to be a local is to be friendly, as most Cypriots are. This applies particularly to the male in the Greek part of the island, and sometimes leads to a windfall of attention for visiting females, many of whom do not mind at all. However, matters rarely seem to get out of hand and normally stay at a superficial level.

Nevertheless, it would not be unknown for a woman who had, perhaps, inadvertently broadcast her temporary domicile in casual conversation, to receive an unsolicited gift as early as the next day. It might be a well-feathered partridge, or even a generous helping of *Soujoukko*, dispatched by special emissary (taxi driver) from the high Troodos by a priest of recent aquaintance. Women wishing to avoid this kind of eventuality should display a certain amount of reserve.

On the beach the irritating practice by young men of sitting close to female visitors seems to be less prevalent these days. In any case the intruders will depart if instructed to do so clearly. Fortunately, or unfortunately, for visiting men there is as much chance of harassment from the local women as there is of an earthquake.

CHILDREN

The Cypriots love children and indulge them, and foreign juveniles are immediately at an advantage. Children are welcome everywhere, including bars, tavernas and restaurants. A Greek wedding is like a football match as noisy children race up and down the church during the service. Child molesting is unheard of.

As far as entertainment goes, there are no waterparks or marinelands, although there are some travelling fairs at festivals (see page 104). As the summer weather is so good the beaches and boat trips should suit youngsters if they can avoid sunburn. Walks in the forests around Platres or in the western hills should also be to their liking. Climbing the pathways to the great elevated castles of the Kyrenia hills will also keep their interest (and use up energy). One should not forget the zoo at Limassol and the smaller one in Larnaca. In Nicosia there are

Fishing off the rocks: Cyprus's coast is a paradise for children

several Lunar Parks (fun-fairs), a good one being the Drakoumel at Eleones Street. There is horse-riding at two centres in Cyprus (see **Sport** page 106–7).

Most hotels offer a babysitting service.

TIGHT BUDGET

● The *Guide to Hotels* by the Tourist Office is invaluable.
● Cheap flights are available out of season (though a Cyprus address must be given when booking).
● Last minute bookings for accommodation, especially out of season, can bring reductions. Otherwise, campsites and youth hostels (see **Directory**, pages 110 and 120) are inexpensive and cheap stays can be had for

one or two nights in monasteries.

● Buses are of course the cheapest form of transport and service taxis are considerably cheaper than ordinary taxis.

● Car hire is expensive in the south but cheaper in the Turkish part of the island. Big savings can be made by hunting out the local firms, but even then there is the accident waiver insurance to contemplate, which is not cheap.

● Eating out in simple roadside restaurants and cafés is inexpensive. They offer food at remarkably low prices (though there probably is no toilet!).

● For those staying in apartments or studios the cheapest way to eat is to prepare their own food bought at the local supermarket (try the municipal markets for fruit etc).

● Normally a better rate of exchange for currency is obtained in north Cyprus than at home.

● Windsurfers and waterskiers

Orange Festival: such occasions are very much part of the Cypriot scene

can sometimes save money by negotiating a weekly rate.

SPECIAL EVENTS

Greek

January
New Year's Day (1 January) An important day to Greek Cypriots. There is dancing and singing after the New Year's Eve church service and the celebrations run well into the morning.

Epiphany (6 January) In seaside towns, after the church service the priest heads a procession to the water's edge. After a blessing, a replica cross is thrown into the sea and youngsters dive into the icy waters to try and retrieve it.

February/March
Green Monday (also known as Clean Monday) The celebration is a survivor of an old Dionysian festival. It is held on the first day of Lent and the people go out in the country to picnic.

Carnival *(Apokreo)* Takes place during the week preceding Lent

and lasts for 11 days. Limassol hosts the main event, lesser festivities taking place in Paphos. It is a colourful affair of parades and fancy dress.

Greek National Day (25 March) A major religious holiday with processions in the towns.

March/April

Easter A big occasion for the Orthodox Church. Solemn mass takes place on Good Friday followed by processions through the streets. After the midnight services on Saturday there are more processions followed by fireworks. Many of the old customs survive, including the 'breaking of the eggs' between friends. On Sunday the Resurrection of Christ is celebrated.

May/June

Labour Day (1 May)

Kataklysmos (late May/early June) Festival of the flood.

Spring Flower Festival or Anthestiria (May) In many parts of the island (especially Paphos) there are flower shows. Chariots parade through the villages decorated with flowers and scenes of Greek mythology.

International State Fair This promotion of trade and commerce is held in Nicosia at the end of May or in early June. Manufactured goods from many countries are displayed against a background of dancing and folk music.

Nicosia Arts Festival (June) Famagusta Gate is the centre of this two-week event. In addition to art there is folk-dancing, ballet and rock music.

St Paul's Feast (29 June) At this religious festival in Paphos the Archbishop officiates in all his Byzantine splendour. The icon of St Paul is then carried through the streets.

August

Assumption Day (15 August)

September

Limassol Wine Festival A 12-day orgy of wine-tasting, eating and dancing to celebrate the island's wine production.

October

Cyprus Independence Day (1 October)

Ochi Day (28 October) Celebrating the Greeks' refusal of Mussolini's demand in 1940 that Italian troops should pass through their territory (*Ochi* means 'no'), the morning is one of marches and flag-carrying.

Turkish

The Turks do not seem to have as much fun as the Greeks. There is the **Children's Festival** on 23 April and the **Youth Festival** on 19 May. See also **Directory,** page 115 for details.

SPORT

Most sports are popular in Cyprus. However, golfers will be disappointed, the only courses as yet being on the British Bases where greens are referred to as 'browns'.

Spectator Sports

Perhaps the biggest international event in the south is the **Cyprus Car Rally**. Held in September, it attracts entries from many countries and includes champion drivers.

Winding mountain roads and rough dirt tracks make it a tough

SPORT

proposition for car and driver.
Football at international level is
played in Limassol's stadium.
Local teams play in the Cyprus
league from October to May.
Tennis The Cypriots are
enthusiastic tennis players. One
important competition is the
Troodos Tennis Tournament held
every year in Troodos (see page
108).
Horse-racing is confined to
Nicosia and the Greek sector.
Race meetings on the flat take
place at weekends and
sometimes mid-week. The course
is near St Paul's Street, Ayios
Dhometios, west of the city.

Activities

Boating
Speed boats can be hired to roar
up and down the coast.
Alternatively, visitors can join a
group for a day's cruising.

Cycling
Bikes can be hired in all the
resorts and many visitors take to
two wheels. However, the official
tourist literature suggests cyclists
should keep off main roads at
weekends because of the volume
of traffic.
The Cyprus Cycling Federation,
20 Ionos Street, Nicosia, tel: (02)
456344, organises competitions
in spring and autumn. Anyone
can take part.

Diving
Spear fishing with aqualung
requires a special licence.
Certified divers can obtain this
without trouble from the District
Fisheries Departments in Nicosia
(tel: (02) 303527), Limassol (tel:
(05) 330470), Larnaca (tel: (04)

The sky's the limit for activities

630294) and Paphos (tel: (06)
240268). Organised sub-aqua
clubs and diving centres can be
found in all the towns and resorts,
as well as at a number of hotels.
In addition various sporting shops
sell or hire equipment.

Fishing
Amateur anglers are welcome to
fish in the sea without a licence
and this includes spear fishing.
There are, however, some
restrictions on the number of
hooks per line and the species of
fish to be caught. Inland anglers
use the many dams and here
licences are required, available
from the appropriate District
Fisheries Department (see
Diving for contact phone
numbers).

Horse-riding
Lapatsa Sports Centre, tel: (02)
621201, near Pano Deftera (about
7 miles/11km southwest of
Nicosia) incorporates a horse-
riding school for beginners up to
advanced level. Open all year
round except Mondays. Five
miles (8km) east of the hotels in

Limassol, at Pareklissa Junction, is Elias Horse Riding Centre, tel: (05) 325000/329444, open all the year (closed 12.30-15.00 hrs daily).

Horses and ponies can be hired for trekking through the Troodos Mountains.

Sailing

Larnaca Marina has berthing facilities for 450 yachts (tel: (04) 653110).

Limassol Sheraton Pleasure Harbour is found by the Sheraton Hotel east of Limassol. It has berths for 227 craft (tel: (05) 321100 ext 3312).

In the north, Kyrenia Marina has berths for 100 craft (tel: (081) 53587).

There are nautical clubs at Limassol, Larnaca, Paphos and Kyrenia as well as inland Nicosia. Less ambitious sailing, although perhaps nearly as much fun, can be had in hired dinghies off any of the beach resorts.

Skiing

Mount Olympus, at 6,401 feet (1,951m) above sea-level, is the only peak in Cyprus that catches the snow. There are four short runs of about 220 yards (200m) in length in Sun Valley. Over on the North Face there are five descents, more demanding and two to three times as long. Good skiers, however, will not find them difficult. For cross-country skiers there are, in theory at least, two tracks 2½ miles (4km) and 5 miles (8km) long. Equipment can be rented at the cabin in Sun Valley 1. On these slopes there are two cafés and another one on the North Face. Ski instruction is available.

At weekends it is as well to get to the slopes early if equipment is wanted.

As competitions are held from time to time at weekends on the North Face, it is worthwhile to check with the Ski Federation in Nicosia, PO Box 2185, Nicosia, tel: (02) 365340 to find out what the situation is when you want to ski there.

The season runs from the first week in January to the end of March and sometimes longer. Vast amounts of snow fall regularly but it melts fairly rapidly when the sun comes out. Nevertheless, proper clothing is a necessity. Powder snow is quite rare.

The slopes can be reached in about an hour from Nicosia and Limassol. Early arrivals might well beat the snow plough and find the last half mile (800m) impassable without wheel chains. For anyone wishing to stay overnight, Troodos has two hotels and Platres several (see page 64). Neither place is up in *après-ski*, but the best hope is Platres.

Swimming

Sea The clear blue Mediterranean waters and long stretches of sandy beach provide excellent opportunities for swimmers and 'bathers' alike. On every beach, red buoys indicate the swimmers' areas. The three Cyprus Tourism Organisation public beaches, all in attractive sites, offer full facilities to swimmers, including changing rooms and beach furniture for hire, as well as beachside refreshment areas. CTO Tourist Assistants supervise the beaches and lifeguards are usually

SPORT

present. Other beaches on the island also provide facilities for swimmers.

Pools Some good open air pools can be found in the main centres. The new Olympic Swimming Pool in Nicosia is the best, but Limassol also has an Olympic-standard pool. Heated outdoor pools also exist in Larnaca and Paphos.

Tennis

Some hotels have tennis courts. The following centres (mostly floodlit) are open to the public:
Nicosia Eleon Tennis Club, 3 Ploutarchos Street, Engomi, tel: (02) 449923. Southwest of the city centre.
Field Club, Egypt Avenue (tel: (02) 452041). Centre of town.
Lapatsa Sporting Centre, Pano Deftera, tel: (02) 621201. 7 miles (11km) southwest of Nicosia.
Limassol Famagusta Tennis Club, 3 Messaorias Street, tel: (05) 335952). Centre of town. Limassol Sporting Club, 11 Olympion Street, tel: (05) 359818. West of the town centre.
Larnaca Larnaca Tennis Club, Kilkis Street, tel: (04) 656999. In the town centre.
Paphos Yeroskipou Public Beach, tel: (06) 234525. 2 miles (3km) east of Paphos.

Walking

Midsummer is much too hot for this pastime; even the mountain temperatures prove too high for most people. The best times are spring and early summer and October. Winter can be wet and cloudy, although there are many good days.
Various marked nature trails exist in the Troodos Mountains and the Akamas peninsula. The Cyprus Tourism Organisation produces a detailed booklet for each area, available free from tourist offices. Other nature trails, through the forested areas of Cape Greco in the Famagusta area, the Troodos (near Agros village), and in the Paphos Forest, have been prepared by the Forestry Department. Ambitious walkers should try the hills south of Palekhori, or the hills overlooking the west coast and the Akamas peninsula. Useful maps to 1:50,000 scale are the United Kingdom Ministry of Defence series, K717. There are restrictions on the sale of these and the Department of Lands and Surveys in Nicosia (tel: (02) 403390) will advise on the latest position. Walkers in the northern hills will have problems of access in some areas because of military camps.

Waterskiing

Boats and skis can be rented at all the main resort areas. The standard of equipment varies; there can also be much waiting around for the right conditions. Fig Tree Bay on the east coast is the best area with some fine runs down the coast.

Windsurfing

All the main beaches have a selection of boards for hire. Winds are rarely strong in summer. Courses of instruction are available. Beginners will waste their time and money if they try to go it alone. Some boards have a sandpaper type of finish and can remove every vestige of skin from hapless learners.

DIRECTORY

Arriving

By Air

In the Greek-controlled part of the island there are two airports (Nicosia airport is under UN control and is not used for commercial flights). Larnaca in the east is three miles (5km) from the town. Paphos airport is out west and nine miles (15km) from the town.

Most visitors require only a passport and this includes citizens of the United Kingdom, Commonwealth countries, the countries of Western Europe and the United States. However, UK nationals who intend travelling to Cyprus via Turkey (not just in transit), will require a visa for that country.

Immigration formalities mean longish queues on arrival but at least you get a stamp in your passport and it allows you to stay for three months. No vaccination or health certificates are required. There are currency controls (see page 116).

Both airports have all the facilities that you would expect, eg duty-free shops, cafés, restaurants, tourist information and hotel reservation service. However, there is only air-conditioning in the lounge at Larnaca making Paphos uncomfortable in summer. Unless visitors are on a package tour, onward transport from the airport is mostly by (metered) taxi.

Flights to north Cyprus arrive at Ercan airport, 23 miles (37km) from Kyrenia and 30 miles (48km) from Famagusta. No airline flies direct, all have to stop in Turkey to comply with formalities. The airport is of the same standard as Larnaca and Paphos. Airport tax is included in the ticket price.

If asked, the immigration officer will agree to forgo the passport stamp. Instead he will stamp a piece of paper which must be retained until departure. A stamp on your passport would prohibit entry at any time into southern Cyprus as the Greek Cypriot government has declared all visitors to the north, with the exception of those passing through the checkpoint in Nicosia, as illegal immigrants. A north Cyprus passport stamp can also cause difficulties for travellers to Greece.

By Boat

Passenger services connect the Republic of Cyprus with Piraeus and Rhodes (Greece), Ancona (Italy), Haifa (Israel), Port Said (Egypt) and Jounieh (Lebanon). Most sailings are from Limassol with a few from Larnaca. Regular services do not commence until the spring. A detailed 'Info-Paper' on ferry boats from the south is available from the Cyprus Tourism Organisation.

In north Cyprus a ferry connects Kyrenia with Tasucu and Mersin in southern Turkey. From Famagusta there is a year-round passenger and car ferry service to Mersin. The operator in both cases is the Cyprus Turkish Maritime Line. As with Ercan airport the immigration officer will forgo the passport stamp if asked (see **Arriving – By Air**).

Camping

This is only permitted in approved sites licensed by the Cyprus Tourism Organisation. At present there are six such sites in the south and the comforts provided include electricity, toilets and showers, food shop and café and washing facilities.

Ayia Napa (tel: (03) 721946). Situated 1¼ miles (2km) west of the town near the beach with a capacity for 150 tents/caravans. Open March – October.

Feggari (tel: (06) 621534). Lies 10 miles (16km) north of Paphos,

near Coral Bay beach. Small with spaces for only 47 tents/caravans. Open all year.

Geroskipou Zenon Gardens, Paphos (tel: (06) 242277) 2 miles (3km) east of Paphos and east of the Public beach with spaces for 95 tents/caravans right by the beach. Open April – October.

Governor's Beach, Pentakomo (tel: (05) 632300). Situated 12½ miles (20km) east of Limassol town. 111 caravans and 247 tents. Open all year.

Polis (tel: (06) 321526). Next to the beach north of the town. A pleasant place among trees, it will take 200 tents/caravans. Open March – October.

Troodos (tel: (05) 421624). This elevated site, at 5,500 feet (1,700 metres) above sea-level and 1¼ miles (2km) from Troodos Hill Resort off the main Troodos – Kakopetria road, is rather basic. Spaces are allocated among the pine trees. Open May – October. A few private sites near beach restaurants and run by the owners, are permitted. The facilities are usually limited. In north Cyprus there is one camp site at **Kyrenia (Riviera Mocamp)** and another at **Famagusta (Onur)**.

Chemist see Pharmacist

Crime

There is not much crime in Cyprus. Any problem in this respect is unlikely to be with the Cypriots for they are generally honest and law abiding. The same cannot be said of every visitor, so reasonable precautions should be taken. For example, the car should be locked, with belongings stored in the boot;

money and jewellery ought to be kept in the hotel safe.

Customs Regulations

In July 1990 Cyprus applied for full membership of the European Community but a decision has yet to made. Customs allowances are to be increased in 1993 for EC member countries, so check with the Cyprus Tourism Organisation for details. The current allowances are:
Tobacco 250 grams (or equivalent in tobacco products, eg 200 cigarettes)
Spirits other than perfumed spirits 1 litre
Wine (one bottle) 0.75 litre
Perfume and toilet water 0.30 litre including one bottle of perfume of not more than 0.15 litre.
Articles of any other description (except jewellery) up to a total value of the equivalent of CY£50.
The above applies to the north and south. However, when a passenger re-enters the Republic of Cyprus (southern Cyprus) after less than 72 hours he is allowed to import duty free only 250 grams of tobacco. For currency controls see page 116.

Disabled Travellers see Senior Citizens

Driving

Traffic keeps to the left, or is supposed to. All drivers should proceed carefully at first until they get the feel of things. For example, red lights in Cyprus do not mean quite the same to everybody; so do not assume that the way is always clear.

● Breakdowns

Towing facilities in the south are provided by the Cyprus Automobile Association in Nicosia (tel: (02) 313131). It is a non-profit making association. Private garage owners can be traced in the yellow pages of the telephone directory under 'Car Cranes'.

● Car Comfort

Cars get unbelievably hot in summer so parked cars should be left with the windows down a fraction. It is worthwhile taking a couple of car blinds. A car fan which plugs into the cigarette lighter and sits on top of the dashboard is another good idea. An air-conditioned car will make life a lot easier all round. Driving west into the setting sun has its problems with dusty windscreens, so it is essential to make sure the screen wash is topped up. In the dark it is best to avoid the less frequented villages as the motorist will become a prisoner in the labyrinthine streets. After rain some roads are dangerously slippery.

● Car Rental

There are many companies, including the internationally known, and cars can be obtained at the airport or in town. Drivers normally need to be at least 21

In the foothills of the Troodos

DIRECTORY

years of age to rent a car (quite often 25), and visitors driving on their own national driving licence must have been in possession of the licence for at least two years. Cars are expensive in the south and cheap in the north. In the high season it may not be possible to get one at short notice. Companies in the Greek-controlled part of the island list four categories of vehicle (below 1,000cc to above 1,300cc). There is the waiver for collision damage to consider. For categories A, B and C it is CY£3 per day, for category D it is CY£4. Without it, the renter is responsible for the first CY£300 and CY£500 respectively for any damage.

In the north there are no less than eleven groups of vehicle ranging from small saloons to air-conditioned jeeps. Some cars rented in the north may have left-hand drive – which can be confusing.

Cars can on occasions be sent out with horribly split tyres, no jack, faulty lights, or poor brakes. A quick check should therefore be made.

● Licence and Insurance
Visitors can drive in Cyprus on

Greek road signs are easy to read

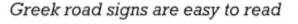

their own national driving licence or an international driving licence. They can bring their own cars for up to three months, but a valid registration document of the car's country of origin is required. Green card insurance is not accepted; insurance must cover Cyprus specifically, otherwise cover should be effected at the port of entry.

Cars, including rented cars, cannot pass between the two sectors of divided Cyprus.

● Petrol
Petrol in the Greek sector costs as much as any in Europe. In the north it is very cheap, about half the cost. Petrol stations are generally open on Saturdays and Sundays between 06.00 and 16.00 (in rural areas there is a rota for Sundays and holidays). At other times they close about 18.00 hours.

● Roads and Speed Limits
Most roads are at least fairly good (less so in the north), although a few are so narrow that two wheels have to be put off the asphalt when meeting oncoming traffic. The road between Limassol and Nicosia is a broad highway approaching motorway standard, although not on entry and exits. A speed limit of 62mph (100kph) operates on this road, 49mph (80kph) on the others out of the towns. In the south, international road traffic signs are used and speed limits are posted in kilometres per hour; in the north, signs are in Turkish and speed limits in miles per hour. Secondary mountain roads are very slow going with their

succession of hairpin bends. Dirt roads are even worse and should be avoided unless there is absolutely no alternative. Traffic in the towns is fairly orderly. Here the speed limit is 31mph (50kph), or less where indicated.

● **Seat Belts**
In both sectors seat belts are compulsory for front seat passengers, also children under five cannot sit in the front seats. From five to ten years children in the front must have an appropriate child's belt.

Electricity
The supply is 240 volts AC and socket outlets in most modern buildings are for three-pin square plugs. Adaptors are available in local hotels and shops. Apartments and hotels generally have a 110 volt outlet for shavers.

Embassies and Consulates
(As north Cyprus is only recognised by Turkey these are all in the south).

British High Commission, Alexander Pallis Street, Nicosia (tel: (02) 473131/7).

Australian High Commission, 4 Annis Komninis Street, 2nd Floor, corner of Stassinos Avenue, Nicosia (tel: (02) 473001).

Canadian High Commission, 4 Queen Frederica Street, Suite 101, Nicosia (tel: (02) 459830).

US Embassy, Dositheos and Therissos Streets, Lycavitos, Nicosia (tel: (02) 465151).

Emergency Telephone Numbers

South
In case of emergency, immediate response will be given by telephoning the following numbers:

Ambulance: 199 (all towns)
Fire Service: 199 (all towns)
Police: 199 (all towns)
Night Pharmacies: 192
  (all towns)

General Hospitals:
  Nicosia (02) 451111
  Limassol (05) 330156
  Larnaca (04) 630322
  Paphos (06) 240111
  Paralimni (03) 821211
  Polis (06) 321431
  Kyperounta (02) 532021

North
Police
  Nicosia (Lefkosa) (020) 83411
  Kyrenia (Girne) (081) 52014
  Famagusta (Gazimagusa) (036) 65310
First Aid
  Nicosia (020) 71441
  Kyrenia (081) 52266
  Famagusta (036) 62876

Entertainment Information
In the south the Cyprus Tourism Organisation (CTO) issues a *Monthly Events* guide which can be obtained at hotels and tourist offices on the island. It also issues a *Diary of Events* which lists the entire year's organised activities and this can be obtained at the Tourist Offices in Cyprus and abroad.

Entry Formalities see Arriving

DIRECTORY

Entry into North Cyprus from the South

Since November 1983, travel across the border has been restricted. There is only one point of access along the entire 85-mile (137km) dividing line. This is at the old Ledra Palace hotel (now under UN control) in Nicosia on the west side of the walled city.

The journey across the 'Green Line' is from the south only and is for one day at a time and you must be back by 18.00 hours (sunset in winter). Passports are required and the procedure is to obtain clearance from the police at the Greek checkpoint and then walk through to the Turkish side. Here there is some form-filling to confirm you recognise Turkish occupation, and payment of CY£1. People wishing to go further afield than Nicosia can take a taxi to Kyrenia and/or Famagusta (or other places), or go by bus or rented car. The Turkish Cypriot authorities, if asked, may say that the latter is not possible without notice, so it is best to try the car rental companies direct. It may also be suggested that some tourist sites are not accessible, even though people already in the north visit them freely. Rented cars are not allowed through the checkpoint.

Health Matters

There are no inoculation requirements and no health certificates are needed. Generally, medical facilities must be paid for and visitors are strongly advised to take out private medical insurance. General hospitals have casualty departments for emergency cases. Hotels will make arrangements for medical services upon request.

Private doctors' surgery hours are (weekdays) 09.00-13.00 and 16.00-19.00 hrs.

Cyprus has a healthy climate and the water is safe to drink. It is good practice to wash all fruit. Dogs and sheep are unwitting agents in the development of the life cycle of a parasite that causes a stomach cyst. If passed on to man it has serious consequences and this is the reason why the Cyprus dog population is strictly controlled (although not as much as it used to be and certainly less so in the north). Most dog owners will have a certificate to say their pet is clear; nevertheless, it is good practice to avoid the attentions of licking dogs. Mosquitoes are sometimes a problem and can keep people awake all night. If the room is air-conditioned, kill them before retiring and keep the windows closed. Where windows are of necessity wide open, then a mosquito coil or other proprietary device can be tried. Some people use a mosquito net.

Holidays, Public

Greek

New Year's Day: 1 January
Epiphany Day: 6 January
Green Monday (50 days before Greek Orthodox Easter): variable
Greek National Day: 25 March
Greek Cypriot National Day: 1 April
Good Friday (Greek Orthodox Church): variable
Easter Sunday (Greek Orthodox Church): variable

Easter Monday (Greek
Orthodox Church): variable
Labour day: 1 May
Kataklysmos (Festival of the
Flood): variable
Assumption Day: 15 August
Cyprus Independence Day:
1 October
Greek National Day (Ochi Day):
28 October
Christmas Day: 25 December
Boxing Day: 26 December

Turkish
Children's Festival: 23 April
Spring and Labour Day: 1 May
Youth Festival: 19 May
Peace and Liberty Day: 20 July
Victory Day: 30 August
Turkish National Day: 29
October
Turkish Cypriot National Day:
15 November
The main Muslim holidays –
Bayram at the end of the
Ramadan fast (three days) the
four-day Kurban Bayram and the
Birthday of the Prophet – move
through the lunar calendar.

All public services, private
enterprises and shops are
officially closed on public
holidays. In resort and coastal
areas, however, shops and
certain services remain open.
Some archaeological sites and
museums also remain open (see
Opening Times pages 116–18).

Lost Property
The Cypriots are honest and lost
items may be quickly returned to
their owners. Failing that, the
local police station should be
tried. The loss of insured items
and travellers' cheques should
also be immediately reported to
the responsible authority.

The Cyprus Museum in Nicosia

Media

Newspapers
Greek Cyprus has an incredible
11 daily newspapers plus three
weekly ones. The daily *Cyprus
Mail* is in English and so is the
Cyprus Weekly. English and other
European newspapers are on
sale one day late. In the Turkish
part of Cyprus they have their
own *Cyprus Mail* and this is in
English as is the weekly *Cyprus
Today* and two monthly
magazines.

Radio
Three radio channels are
beamed from the south but only
'Programme Two' (AM 603
KH_z/498 mtrs and VHF/FM 94.8
MH_z) broadcasts in English (as
well as Turkish, Armenian and
Arabic). The English programme
gives news bulletins and weather
forecasts followed by classical
and popular music. From June to
September a tourist programme
called *Welcome to Cyprus* is
broadcast on all days except
Sunday. This is in five languages
and covers a comprehensive
weather forecast and information
on what to see and do. The
English programme starts at
08.30 hrs. BFBS, the British Forces
Broadcasting Service, is on the

air for 24 hours. There are two channels: Channel 1 – 92.1 FM (Akrotiri area), 99.6 FM (Dhekelia area); 89.7 FM (Nicosia area); Channel 2 – 89.9 FM (Akrotiri), 95.3 FM (Dhekelia), 91.9 FM (Nicosia). The programmes are aimed at the Forces personnel and cover many interesting matters as well as news. There are also the BBC World Service programmes. North Cyprus of course can tune into all the above stations, as well as its own.

Television
Programmes transmitted from the south are broadcast every evening and run from 16.00 or 17.00 hrs (12.00 hrs on Sunday) to midnight. The entertainment is in colour and includes material from Britain and America, using the original language and Greek subtitles. Cyprus television is linked with Eurovision for live transmission of major athletic and other events. Stations from Greece and Turkey are also received.

Money Matters
The currency of the Republic (south Cyprus) is the Cyprus pound (CY£) which is divided into 100 cents. Notes in circulation are CY£20, CY£10, CY£5, CY£1 and 50 cents, and coins are 1, 2, 5, 10, 20 and 50 cents.
The Cyprus pound is not traded internationally, its only market maker being the Central Bank of Cyprus. Daily rates against the $US and three other currencies are quoted by the Central Bank. The currency in use in northern Cyprus is the Turkish lira (abbreviated to TL). Coins in circulation are for TL 50, 100, 500 and 1,000; notes are for values up to TL 100,000.

Currency Regulations
Visitors to the Republic can import up to CY£50 in local currency, with no limit on the amount imported in foreign currency of its negotiable equivalent (eg travellers' cheques). Amounts of foreign exchange in excess of the equivalent of $US1,000 should be declared at Customs on form D(NR). Foreign exchange may be re-exported on production at customs of the form D(NR). Visitors can export up to CY£50 in Cyprus currency. Unspent currency originally imported and declared at Customs on arrival and unspent imported cheques, travellers' cheques, etc (not having been converted into Cyprus pounds) can also be exported.
There is no restriction on the amount of currency that can be taken into north Cyprus.

Banks
In addition to the normal opening from Monday to Friday, in the main tourist areas in the south, banks provide afternoon tourist services on Monday and Wednesday to Friday. There is also a night service by the banks at the airports of Larnaca and Paphos.
For banking hours see **Opening Times** below.

Opening Times

South
Shops/Businesses. Summer (1 May – 30 September) Monday,

Tuesday, Thursday, Friday 08.00
– 13.00 and 16.00 – 19.00 hrs,
Wednesday and Saturday 08.00 –
13.00 hrs. Winter (1 October – 30
April) Monday, Tuesday ,
Thursday, Friday 08.00 – 13.00
and 14.30 – 17.30 hrs,
Wednesday and Saturday 08.00 –
13.00 hrs.

Banks. Monday to Friday 08.15 –
12.30 hrs (and 15.30 – 17.30 hrs
Monday and Wednesday to
Friday in the main tourist areas).

Post Offices. Monday to Friday
07.30 – 13.30 hrs (and 15.00 –
18.00 hrs Thursday). Some offices
are open in the afternoon (except
Wednesday) and Saturday
mornings.

Public Services. Monday to
Friday 07.30 – 14.30 hrs (and
15.00 – 18.00 hrs Thursday,
1 September – 30 June).

**Museums, Archaeological Sites
and Historic Buildings**. Times
are all different. Many of the
museums are closed on Sunday
although most of the
archaeological sites are open
every day. Refer to the main text
for the times of the listed
museums and sites. On Greek
Easter Sunday all museums in
Cyprus are closed. Summer

hours mainly apply from 1 June to
30 September. A small charge for
admission is usually made at
most of the museums and
controlled sites.

North
Shops. Summer 07.30 – 13.00
and 16.00 – 18.00 hrs, winter
08.00 – 13.00 and 14.00 – 18.00
hrs.
Early closing on Saturday and
closed on Sunday. In some tourist
resorts shops remain open
throughout the day, sometimes as
late as 20.00 hrs.

Offices/Businesses. Summer
07.30 – 14.00 hrs. Winter 08.00
– 13.00 and 14.00 – 17.00 hrs.
Closed on Saturday and Sunday.

Banks. Monday to Friday 09.00 –
16.00 hrs.

Post Offices. 08.00 – 13.00 and
14.00 – 17.00 hrs, Saturday 08.30
– 12.30 hrs.

**Museums, Archaeological Sites
and Historic Buildings**. Summer
09.00 – 13.30 and 16.30 – 18.30
hrs, winter 08.00 – 13.00 and
14.30 – 17.00 hrs.
Museums are open Tuesday to
Saturday. They are closed in the

Banks are open in the mornings

DIRECTORY

morning on religious holidays and all day on 1 January, 19 May, 29 October and 15 November. Summer hours apply 1 May to 30 September.

Most archaeological sites and historic buildings are open every day and some are accessible even when closed.

Personal Safety

There is at least one type of venomous snake in Cyprus. This is the viper and it is identified by its distinctive zigzag markings. It is unlikely to be encountered, but walkers and climbers in the hills, especially the Kyrenia range, need to watch out. The bite of the snake can kill a dog in half an hour, so if bitten, stay calm and go quickly to the nearest hospital or clinic. A serum is available for those who wish to carry it and feel confident to use it.

Pharmacists

Pharmacies are open during normal shopping hours. Names, addresses and telephone numbers of pharmacies that stay open throughout the night, Sundays and public holidays are listed in the daily papers. They can also be reached in the south by telephoning 192. Some drugs

Villagers rely on the local bus

available only on prescription in most countries are available over the counter.

Photography

In both sectors of Cyprus most of the very popular brands and types of film can be obtained. Film should not be bought from kiosks as it may well have been roasted. Less well known, but by no means obscure, varieties of film cannot easily be obtained, nor can batteries for SLR cameras. In both the south and north there are certain 'restricted areas' for photographers. Photography is forbidden near military camps or other military installations, in museums and in churches with mural paintings and icons where flash is required.

Places of Worship

The religion of the Greek Cypriots is Greek Orthodox. Churches are numerous in the villages as well as the towns. There are Roman Catholic and Armenian churches in Nicosia, Limassol and Larnaca and a Maronite church in Nicosia. There is also a Roman Catholic church in Paphos. Anglican churches are located as follows:
Nicosia: St Paul's, 2 Grigori Afxentiou Street (tel: (02) 442241) (services: Sunday 07.30 and 09.30 hrs)
Limassol: St Barnabas, 177 Leontios Street (tel: (05) 362713) (service: Sunday 09.00 hrs)
Paphos: Chrysopolitissa Church, Kato Paphos (tel: (06) 247970) (service: Sunday 18.00 hrs)
Larnaca: St Helena's, St Helena Building, Flat 201 (tel: (04) 622327).

Police

The police are generally relaxed and helpful and it is claimed that all speak English. Foreigners and pretty women can escape charges for traffic offences if they plead ignorance and smile a lot. If you get into trouble, CTO Tourist Assistants are in charge of areas frequented by visitors and are ready to provide assistance. In an emergency dial 199.

Post Office

There are main post offices in all the towns and sub-post offices in the suburbs. In general, post offices close in the afternoons (see **Opening Times**). Airmail letters take three to four days to Europe. There is a private courier service that gives a next-day or sooner service. Intelpost service is also available for the quick despatch of business documents. The following offices have *poste restante* facilities and an afternoon service.
Nicosia: Eleftheria Square
Limassol: 3 Gladstone Street
Larnaca: King Paul Square
Paphos: Nikodemou Mylona Street.
Postage stamps can be bought at hotels and with postcards at shops.
All mail to and from north Cyprus has to be routed via Turkey.

Public Transport

Buses

Inter-city and village buses operate frequently between the main towns and various holiday resorts with numerous trips per day. Almost all villages are connected by local buses to the nearest towns but services operate only on weekdays once a day (early in the morning and returning to the villages in the afternoon).
Urban and suburban buses operate frequently only during the day, between 05.30 and 19.00 hrs. During summer, in certain tourist areas, bus services operate until midnight. In the south the central city bus stations are at:
Nicosia: Dionysos Solomos Square, west of Eleftheria Square (tel: (02) 473414).
Larnaca: bus stops for all buses along Hermes Street (tel: (04) 650477).
Limassol: between the market and Anexartisias Street (tel: (05) 370592).
Paphos: 'Pervola' bus station, Thermopyles Street (tel: (06) 234252).

Taxis

Service Taxis *(Dolmus)* (shared with other people; 4-7 seats). The service taxi is available between main towns (Nicosia, Limassol, Larnaca and Paphos) usually every half hour from 05.45 – 18.30 hrs (19.30 in summer); Sunday and public holidays 07.00 – 17.30 hrs (18.30 in summer). There is no service between the airport and the towns or between the towns and villages. Seats may be booked by phone. Passengers can be collected from, and dropped at any place within the municipal boundaries. Tariffs vary according to destination.
Rural Taxis Available in hill resorts and other villages (Lefkara, Platres, Kakopetria, Pedhoulas, Agros, etc).
Urban Taxis Available in all the towns in the south; charge by

DIRECTORY

meter. For hiring a taxi between 23.00 and 06.00 hrs an additional 15 per cent on the amount indicated on the meter is charged. For any piece of luggage weighing more than 12 kilos there is an additional charge.

There is no **railway system**.

Senior Citizens

Few concessions are made to elderly visitors or the disabled. Most villages and many parts of towns lack a complete pavement. Hotels have no ramps, steps are everywhere.

Public telephones, old and new

Student and Youth Travel

Cyprus is not on the backpacker's route. There is no such thing as a really cheap air fare and budget accommodation is limited. There are some campsites (see page 110) and the following youth hostels:

Nicosia: 5 Hadjidaki Street (off Themistoklis Dervis Street). *Open:* 07.30 – 23.00 hrs. Tel: (02) 444808.

Larnaca: 27 Nicolaou Rossou Street (near St Lazarus Church). *Open:* 07.30 – 22.00 hrs. Tel: (04) 442027.

Limassol: 120 Ankara Street (behind Limassol Castle). Tel: (05) 363749. (Temporarily closed for renovation.)

Paphos: 37 Eleftherias Venizelos Avenue. *Open:* 07.30 – 22.00 hrs. Tel: (06) 232588.

Troodos: 400m from Troodos Square on Kakopetria Road. *Open:* 07.30-10.30 and 16.00-22.00 hrs April to October. Tel: (05) 421649.

Stavros tis Psokas Rest House, Paphos Forest, tel: (06) 722338 (advance reservation essential).

Telephones

Cyprus is connected by automatic dialling systems to many countries. In the south, coin-operated call boxes are installed in all towns and many villages as well as at the airports. Instructions for making calls are displayed. Coins accepted include 2, 10 and 20 cent pieces, new phones also accept 5 cent pieces.

The international code for the UK is 0044; Eire 00353; US and Canada 001; Australia 0061; New Zealand 0064; followed by the town code (number minus the initial zero) then the number. Codes in Cyprus are: (South) Nicosia 02; Limassol 05; Larnaca 04; Paphos 06; Ayia Napa 03. (North) Nicosia (Lefkosa) 020; Kyrenia (Girne) 081; Famagusta (Gazimagusa) 036.

For telephone enquiries dial 192 in all towns.

Time

Cyprus is two hours ahead of GMT; in summer clocks are put forward one hour.

Tipping

The burden of tipping is taken care of in cafés and restaurants, for the bill usually (but not always) comes complete with a 10 per cent service charge and nothing extra need be offered. Service at small cafés in the north is given without the expectation of a tip.

Drinks at the bar produce a bill with each round (not in the north) but payment in many places is not until departure. If no service charge has been added then a reasonable but not extravagant tip should be left. Before mass tourism, taxi drivers did not expect a tip but wear an air of expectancy now.

Toilets

The modern hotels have wonderful lavatories. However, public toilets are rare. Cafés and bars in the northern resorts have acceptable toilets. Roadside cafés at the edge of town, and restaurants under the trees often have primitive facilities.

To the surprise of many, the waste paper basket by the WC is to collect used toilet paper; otherwise the drains will block.

Tourist Offices

South

Main office (postal enquiries only) 19 Limassol Avenue, Nicosia, PO Box 4535, tel: (02) 315715.
Nicosia: Laiki Yitonia (east of Eleftheria Square), tel: (02) 444264.
Limassol: 15 Spyros Araouzos Street, tel: (05) 362756, and 35 George A'Street (opposite west entrance Dhassoudi Beach) in Potamos tis Yermassoyias area, tel: (05) 323211.

Larnaca: Vasileos Pavlou Square, tel: (04) 654322.
Paphos: 3 Gladstone Street, tel: (06) 232841.
Ayia Napa: 17 Archbishop Makarios Avenue, tel: (03) 721796.
Platres: (April to October only), tel: (05) 421316.
There are also offices at Larnaca and Paphos airports and Limassol harbour.
Offices are open every morning except Sunday, and on Monday and Thursday afternoon.

North

Nicosia (Lefkosa): tel: (020) 75051.
Kyrenia (Girne) Harbour: tel: (081) 52145.
Famagusta (Gazimagusa): tel: (036) 62864.

Offices Abroad

UK: Cyprus Tourist Office, 213 Regent Street, London W1R 8DA (tel: 071-734 9822).
UK: North Cyprus Tourist Office, 28 Cockspur Street, London SW1Y 5BN (tel: 071-930 5069).
US: Cyprus Tourism Organisation, 13 East 40th Street, New York 10016 (tel: (212) 683-5280).

Travel Agents

There are about 290 licensed travel agencies in operation in Cyprus. Many are IATA members. The association of Cyprus Travel Agents, PO Box 2369 Nicosia can be contacted by telephone on (02) 366435. In the north the main agent is CTA, and they have offices in Nicosia, Kyrenia and Famagusta. The *Guide to Hotels, Travel Agencies and other Tourist Services* is available from the CTO.

LANGUAGE

Cyprus always had two official languages, Greek and Turkish. The present division of the island means that Greek is spoken in the south and Turkish in the north. There is no need for English speakers to learn Greek, for many Greek Cypriots, including all those in the tourist industry that the visitor is likely to meet, speak good English. Where an attempt at the language is useful is in the village coffee shop and similar places, for here it will most likely lead to further conversation and the locals may know no English. In the north things are somewhat different. There is not as much English spoken. Waiters and others often have only a limited fluency and some knowledge of Turkish is a definite advantage.

Greek

Unless you know the Greek script, a vocabulary is not of very much use to the visitor. But it is helpful to know the alphabet, so that you can find your way around; and the following few basic words and phrases will help too. (See also **Food and Drink** page 95).

Alphabet

Alpha	Αα	short a, as in hat
Beta	Ββ	v sound
Gamma	Γγ	guttural g sound
Delta	Δδ	hard th, as in father
Epsilon	Εε	short e
Zita	Ζζ	z sound
Eta	Ηη	long e, as in feet
Theta	Θθ	soft th, as in think
Iota	Ιι	short i, as in hit
Kappa	Κκ	k sound
Lambda	Λλ	l sound
Mu	Μμ	m sound
Nu	Νν	n sound
Xi	Ξξ	x or ks sound
Omicron	Οο	short o, as in pot
Pi	Ππ	p sound
Rho	Ρρ	r sound
Sigma	Σσ	s sound
Taf	Ττ	t sound
Ipsilon	Υυ	another ee sound, or y as in funny
Phi	Φφ	f sound
Chi	Χχ	guttural ch, as in loch
Psi	Ψψ	ps, as in chops
Omega	Ωω	long o, as in bone

Numbers

1 éna
2 dío
3 tría
4 téssera
5 pénde
6 éxi
7 eptá
8 októ
9 ennía
10 déka
11 éndeka
12 dódeka
13 dekatría
14 dekatéssera
15 dekapénde
16 dekaéxi
17 dekaeptá
18 dekaokto
19 dekaennía
20 ikosi
30 triánda
40 saránda
50 penínda
100 ekató
101 ekaton éna
1000 chília

Basic Vocabulary

good morning kaliméra
good evening kalispéra
goodnight kaliníkta
goodbye chérete

hello yásou
thank you efcharistó
please/you're welcome parakaló
yes ne
no óchi
where is . . .? poo íne?
how much is . . .? póso káni?
I would like tha íthela
do you speak English? milate
  angliká?
I don't speak Greek then miló
  helliniká

Places
street ódos
avenue léofóros
square platía
restaurant estiatório
hotel xenodochío
room domátio
post office tachithromío
letter grámma
stamps grammatóssima
police astinomía
customs teloniakos
passport diavatírion
pharmacy farmakío
doctor iatrós
dentist odontiatrós
entrance isothos
exit éxothos
bank trápeza
church eklisía
hospital nosokomío
café kafeneion

Travelling
car aftokínito
bus leoforío
boat karávi
garage garáz
bus station stasi ton leoforío
airport aerodrómio
ticket isitírio

Food and Drink
food fagitó
bread psomí
water neró

wine krasí
beer bira
coffee kafé

Fish
lobster astakós
squid kalamarákia
octopus oktapóthi
red mullet barboúnia
whitebait marithes
sea bream sinagrítha

Meat/Poultry
lamb arnáki
chicken kotópoulo
meat balls kefthédes
meat on a skewer souvlákia
liver sikóti

Vegetables
spinach spanáki
courgette kolokithia
beans fasólia

Salads and Starters
olives eliés
yoghurt and cucumber dip tzatsiki
tomato and cucumber salad angour
  domata
stuffed vine leaves dolmades
'Greek' salad with cheese horiatiki

Desserts
honeycake baklavá
honey puffs loukoumádes
semolina cake halvá
ice cream pagotó
yoghurt yiaourti
shredded wheat and honey kataifi
custard tart bougatsa

Turkish
The Turkish alphabet is very similar to
the Latin alphabet except for a few
letters which have special
pronunciation:

$C =$ j as in *Cami* (mosque),
  pronounced Jami

LANGUAGE

ç = ch as in *Foça*, pronounced Focha

g = unpronounced but serves to extend the preceding vowel, so that *dag* (mountain) is pronounced Daa

Ö = oe as in *Göreme*, pronounced Goereme

s = sh as in *Kusadasi,* pronounced Kushadasi

ü = like the French 'tu', as in *Ürgüp*

i = pronounced like the 'a' in the English word 'serial'

Everyday Phrases

hello merhaba

goodbye allahaismarladik (said by the person leaving) gule gule (said by the person seeing his or her friend off)

good morning gunaydin

good evening iyi aksamlar

goodnight iyi geceler

please lutfen

thank you tesekkur ederim, or mersi

yes evet

no hayir

there is var

there is not yok

how are you? nasilsiniz

I am well, thank you iyiyim, tesekkur ederim

Numbers

1 bir
2 iki
3 uc
4 dort
5 bes
6 alti
7 yedi
8 sekiz
9 dokuz
10 on
11 on bir
20 yirmi
30 otuz
40 kirk
50 elli
60 altmis
70 yetmis
80 seksen
90 doksan
100 yuz
101 yuz bir
200 iki yuz
300 uc yuz
1000 bin
2000 iki bin

The Time and the Days

when? nezaman?

yesterday dun

today bugun

tomorrow yarin

morning sabah

afternoon ogleden sonra

evening aksam

night gece

one hour bir saat

what is the time? saat kac?

at what time? saat kacta?

Sunday Pazar

Monday Pazartesi

Tuesday Sali

Wednesday Carsamba

Thursday Persembe

Friday Cuma

Saturday Cumartesi

While Travelling

airport hava alani

port liman

town centre sehir Merkezi

where is it? nerede?

is it far? uzak mi?

tourism bureau turizm burosu

repair garage bir tamirci

a good hotel iyi bir otel

a restaurant bir lokanta

In the Hotel

a room bir oda

two people iki kisi

a room with a bathroom banyolu bir oda

what is the price? fiyati nedir?

hot water sicak su

supplementary bed ilave bir yatak

breakfast kahvalti

butter tereyag

coffee kahve
tea cay
milk sut
sugar seker
the bill hesap

Shopping
gold altin
silver gumus
leather deri
copper bakir
how much is it? bu ne kadar?

In the Restaurant
bread ekmek
water su
mineral water madensuyu
fruit juice meyva suyu
wine sarap
beer bira
ice buz
meat et
mutton koyun eti
lamb kuzu eti
beef sigir eti
veal dana eti
chicken pilic
fish balik

Hor's d'oeuvre (mezeler)
spicy fried liver
  with onions arnavut cigeri
cold chicken in walnut
  purée with garlic cerkez tavugu
spicy raw meatballs cig kofte
fish-roe salad tarama
stuffed vine leaves yaprak dolmasi

Soups (corbalar)
yoghurt soup yogurt corbasi
meat soup with egg yolks dugun
  corbasi
tripe soup iskembe corbasi

Grills (izgaralar)
fillet steak bonfile
lamb grilled on a revolving
  spit doner kebap
lamb chops pirzola
grilled lamb on skewers sis kebap
grilled meatballs sis kofte

Pilafs
plain rice pilaf sade pilav
rice with pine nuts, currants
  and onions ic pilav
cracked wheat pilaf bulgur pilav

Cold vegetables in olive oil
split aubergine with
  tomatoes and onions imam bayildi
fried baby marrow served
  with yoghurt kabakkizartmasi
fried aubergine slices with
  yoghurt patlican kizartmasi
green beans in tomato
  sauce zeytinyagli fasulye

Savoury pastries (borekler)
fried filo pastry filled with
  cheese sigara boregi
layers of filo pastry filled
  with cheese or meat su boregi
puff pastry filled with meat talas

Salads (salatalar)
chopped cucumber in
  garlic-flavoured yoghurt cacik
mixed tomato, pepper,
  cucumber and onion coban salatasi
puréed aubergine salad patlican
  salatasi
haricot bean and onion
  salad piyaz

Desserts (tatlilar)
flaky pastry stuffed with nuts
  in syrup baklava
shredded wheat stuffed with
  nuts and syrup tel kadayif
cold rice pudding sutlac
cold stewed fruit komposto
ice cream dondurma

Fruits (meyvalar)
grapes uzam
peaches seftali
plums erik
apricots kayisi
cherries kiraz
figs incir
yellow melon kavun
water melon karpuz

INDEX

INDEX/ACKNOWLEDGEMENTS

ACKNOWLEDGEMENTS

The Automobile Association would like to thank the following photographers and libraries for their assistance in the preparation of this book

ROBERT BULMER AND ROY RAINFORD took all the photographs (©AA Photo Library) except those listed below and thank Kodak Films for their assistance.

J ALLAN CASH PHOTO LIBRARY
75 Othello's Tower, Famagusta.

INTERNATIONAL PHOTOBANK
Front cover Paphos harbour, 4 Kykko Monastery, 8 Kourion ruined temple, 12 Paphos castle & harbour, 13 Ayia Napa fishing harbour, 20 Stavrovouni Monastery, 31 Lefkara, 33 Rock of Aphrodite, Paphos, 35 Pelican.

NATURE PHOTOGRAPHERS LTD
85 Cape Greco (N A Callow), 86 Cyprus Warbler (M Gore), 89 Cyprus bee orchid (D M Turner Ettinger), 90 Two-tailed pasha butterfly (S C Bisserott), 93 Cyprus moufflon (M Gore).

SPECTRUM COLOUR LIBRARY
23 Boats, Limassol, 58 Selimiye Mosque, 77 Ruins of St George of the Greeks, 104 Orange Festival.